MW00397368

THE COMPLETE
*Hunter*™

# Black Bear Hunting

## Expert Strategies for Success

Gary Lewis &
Lee Van Tassell

**Creative Publishing**
international

www.creativepub.com

GARY LEWIS is an outdoor writer, speaker and photographer who makes his home in Oregon. He has hunted and fished in five countries on two continents and in much of the American West. His previous books have won national awards and his magazine articles have appeared in magazines such as *Sports Afield*, *Traditional Bowhunter*, *Bear Hunting* and *Mule Deer*.

LEE VAN TASSELL makes his home in Central Oregon. A lifetime hunter, Van Tassell spent four years in South Africa, where he pursued plains game with a rifle. He specializes in spot-and-stalk tactics and calling for big black bears. In over 20 years experience hunting black bears in the Pacific Northwest, he has tagged 28 bears.

**Creative Publishing international**

Copyright © 2007 by Creative Publishing international, Inc.
18705 Lake Drive East
Chanhassen, MN 55317
1-800-328-3895
www.creativepub.com

*799.277*
*Lew*

*President/CEO:* Ken Fund
*VP for Sales & Marketing:* Peter Ackroyd
*Publisher:* Winnie Prentiss
*Executive Managing Editor:* Barbara Harold
*Production Managers:* Laura Hokkanen, Linda Halls
*Creative Director:* Michele Lanci-Altomare
*Senior Design Manager:* Brad Springer
*Design Managers:* Jon Simpson, Mary Rohl
*Cover & Book Design:* Brad Springer
*Page Layout:* Tina R. Johnson

*Printed in Singapore*
10 9 8 7 6 5 4 3 2 1

## BLACK BEAR HUNTING
by Gary Lewis and Lee Van Tassell

All photos © Gary Lewis except:
*Contributing Photographers:* Tom Christie, Mark Emery, Wayne Endicott, Gary Kramer, Mike Martell, Mark Raycroft, Chad Schearer

*Contributing Manufacturers:* Alpen, Austin & Halleck, Bear Near, Bear Scent, LLC, Blackhawk, Buck Bomb, Bushnell, CVA, Federal Ammunition, Fox Pro, Gerber Legendary Blades, Hodgdon, New Line Products, Nosler, Inc., Power Belt Bullets, Quake Industries, Ruger, Security Equipment Corporation, Warne Scope Mounts.

Library of Congress Cataloging-in-Publication Data
Lewis, Gary
  Black bear hunting : expert strategies for success / Gary Lewis, Lee Van Tassell.
       p. cm. -- (The complete hunter)
Includes index.
  ISBN-13: 978-1-58923-315-7 (hard cover)
  ISBN-10: 1-58923-315-8 (hard cover)
  1. Black bear hunting.  I. Van Tassell, Lee II. Title. III. Series.
  SK295.L49 2007
  799.2'7785--dc22                          2006034146

# CONTENTS

# FOREWORD

by Rick Jamison

I had been hunting for black bear in Western Oregon without success when Lee Van Tassell offered to take me along and see what we could do about correcting the unfortunate situation. Soon, I was headed out with Lee and Brian Clark for a weekend in Lee's pickup camper. We arrived at one of Lee's spots in the Coast Range about mid-afternoon and immediately started a hike along an old logging road to see if we could locate a blackie somewhere in the surrounding canyons and mountainsides.

Lee periodically walked to the edge of a canyon to listen for bear activity or to scan the area with binoculars. After a mile or so Brian took up a post to scrutinize a hillside with his binoculars. After a long spell Brian spotted a small sliver of black far below that moved slightly. This was all that was visible of what later materialized into a black bear. Brian summoned me over and after detailed directions and a long search I finally spotted the right speck of black with my binoculars. After a long wait it moved slightly, revealing that it was a bear. I took a rest over a stump with my rifle and waited, watching through the scope. Finally, the bear moved, exposing a bit more of itself. I quickly squeezed the trigger and expected a dead bear to follow. All I got was a quick look at a black blob rapidly departing the overgrown clearcut. After a long walk through thick brush in country steeper than a cow's face we made a careful search to verify that I had not shot any part of the bear.

Back up in the open, I set up a paper plate with a safe backstop and checked the rifle's zero, hoping for an alibi that would redeem my reputation for shooting. I quickly found that the rifle's zero was no alibi. It was dead-on.

That night in camp I lamented the fact that I had completely blown what was probably the only chance I would have. I underestimated Lee's bear-finding ability.

Early the next morning we struck out on foot along another logging road. After half a mile or so we rounded a bend along a mountainside and there was a big bear little more than a hundred yards away! He was intent on eating and had not spotted us. I took careful aim with the .277 Jamison and sent a 130-grain Swift Scirocco into the bear's vitals, then followed with a quick second shot for insurance. My tag was filled, just like that. Next came getting the bear out and to a taxidermist. Along the way, we stopped at a ranch to weigh the bear on a certified scale—325 pounds (146 kg).

After days of searching on my own I had not seen a bear. One evening and morning spent with Lee and I had shot at two! Lee is not only a savvy bear hunter, he's a great guy to be with. You can believe what he says and you would do well to heed his information on bear hunting.

Gary Lewis and Lee Van Tassell have teamed up to bring you a look at bear hunting across North America. They've examined all aspects of the hunt from habitat and scouting to strategies, tactics, tracking and trophy care. They've written the kind of book they felt they needed when they first began hunting bears years ago.

No matter where you hunt black bear, this book has something for you. Gary and Lee take the reader to Prince William Sound and Prince of Wales Island, Alaska and into the mountains and swamps of the Lower 48. In these pages, you'll find the kind of information that gives you the confidence to hunt anywhere that black bear can be found.

*Black Bear Hunting* is the kind of reading that is worth re-reading before each season because this book is written by bear hunters for bear hunters.

– Rick Jamison
May 2007

Hunter, Master Ballistician, Reloading Expert, Editor and Author of *The Rifleman's Handbook: A Shooter's Guide to Reloading, Rifles and Results* and other books

# INTRODUCTION

**U**rsus americanus—the black bear, a predator, an omnivore. To some it is a pest, to others a trophy. To all it is an icon of wilderness and wild country and a life lived on the edge of adventure.

For the pioneer of the eighteenth and ninteenth centuries, the black bear was both bane and bounty. A bear was a nuisance when hungry, and a terror when enraged. It was potential food on the table; the meat was smoked and preserved against starving times; the fat was rendered to grease for fuel or an ingredient in biscuits and pies. The coat made blankets, rugs and robes.

Today's hunter also makes good use of the bear. As stewards of the resource, and as the ultimate predator, our role in nature is to keep animal populations in balance. We control deer numbers to limit the large fluctuations in populations that can strip an area of its browse and hurt the carrying capacity of the land. Similarly, predator control seeks not to eliminate predators, but to keep those populations in check so that prey species are not impacted.

The complete hunter not only hunts for deer, elk, caribou and moose, but does his or her part to control predator populations. Spring and fall bear hunts give the outdoorsman another chance to pursue a passion and go a long way toward keeping the black bear population in check.

Though black bear numbers have declined in some regions in North America as development has taken its toll on wildlife habitat, bear populations are at all-time highs in other areas. On the East Coast, hunting seasons have been instituted where they have been closed for years. It is legal to take bear in spring and fall seasons in many western states and provinces. Restrictions may have tightened in some locales, but the hunting has continued to improve. And in many places, it has never been better.

It's a game of cat and mouse—a high-stakes contest between hunter and hunted, with the elements of chance and advantage on a balance. Make no mistake, the black bear is very one of the most dangerous game species.

Statistics from a USGS study in Alaska bear this out. Between 1980 and 2002, polar bears, which make up 5 percent of the bears in this state, were involved in three recorded attacks which resulted in one fatality and two injuries. Brown and grizzly bears make up 23 percent of the bear population and were involved in 86.3 percent of the conflicts. Black bears, which are thought to number 110,000 across the state to make up 72 percent of the Alaska bear population, were involved in 12.3 percent of the conflicts.

In the Lower 48 states, there are an estimated 2,000 to 3,000 grizzly bears and an approximate

300,000 black bears, which account for most of the bear/human conflicts. In Canada and the U.S., the number of bear/human conflicts is increasing, not because bears are becoming more aggressive, but because there are more people living in and recreating in bear country.

Bear attacks are consistently found to increase in areas where visibility is poor and where the human was alone or separated from a group, which describes the exact behavior exhibited by most hunters.

This is part of the challenge that draws us back to the mountains and the grassy meadows in the spring of the year, or calls us to walk the river banks in the fall. In its purest form, spotting and stalking black bear calls for the hunter to find a vantage point across a canyon, employing optics to search out the cover. When the bear is spotted, the hunter evaluates it at long range. If a decision is made to stalk the animal, hours might pass before the hunter is in range for a shot.

There is nothing easy about hunting the black bear on its own terms. The successful hunter develops a system for evaluating country, for scouting and for using optics. He or she develops skill at setting baits or employing hounds or calling or spotting.

And as the skill grows hunters learns to judge bears and how to stalk quietly into range and shoot. These are the elements that produce consistent results. And this is the system that you'll find in the pages of this book. It is a system for success wherever you hunt black bears.

Those days spent in the forest with binoculars and a bear rifle, or walking the banks of a river when salmon are on the spawning beds, are rare and fine in a hunter's life. With the familiar checkering of the rifle stock comfortable in your hand, the glint of sun on blued metal and oil, the clear, clean air, the expanse of the mountain landscape and every nerve aware—and that's hunting at its best.

# CHAPTER ONE

# Biology of *Ursus americanus*

He walks with a swagger, swinging his head from side to side, lord of his domain. His black hair ripples over powerful shoulders and his tread is soft, his pads and claws leaving wide prints on the trail.

He's a recluse of the northern forest, a seldom-seen denizen of the desert, a predator of great strength and lightning speed and a giant with a sweet tooth. Distributed across most of North America, the black bear is found in huntable numbers in most states and provinces. Yet, he remains a mystery, a shadow in the timber and a challenge to the best big game hunters.

A successful hunter learns the quarry's habits and habitat and recognizes the relationships between the seasons and foods found within the animal's home range.

## BLACK BEAR BASICS

Of the North American bruins, black bears are the smallest. Yet black bears are known to reach weights of 600 pounds (270 kg) and more. An adult bear stands between 29 inches (74 cm) and 36 inches (91 cm) at the shoulder and measures an average of 60 inches (152 cm) from nose to tip of tail. The tail is about 2 inches (5 cm) long. Males, on average, are larger than females. In the spring, an average male weighs 180 to 200 pounds (81 to 90 kg). With a layer of summer fat, a bear may weigh 20 percent more going into its winter den.

Females breed, on average, every other season. Cubs are usually sent packing by June of their second year.

Most people, indeed, most hunters, may never see a black bear in the wild. This is because most bears don't want to be seen. I say most bears, because it is foolish to make blanket statements to describe all black bears. Bears are complex animals and creatures of varied environments, and any given bear may react differently in any given situation. It has been my experience that most bears do not want to be seen by humans.

Most bears are shy. They live in an environment that is largely unfriendly. Occupying a high place on the food chain, they are still prey for several large predators and like to keep the element of surprise on their side. Young cubs are vulnerable to golden eagles, coyotes, mountain lions, wolves and other bears. As they grow older, they are prey to bigger bears and hunters. And even as mature adults, they are subject to disputes with other bears over food, territory or breeding rights. The loser of such a battle may retreat, beaten and bloodied, or end up as dinner.

The size of a bear's range depends on its sex, age and the availability of food. Adult males have much larger ranges than females. According to one study, males may travel over at least 46 square miles (120 square km) during years when food is scarce.

June and July are the primary months of breeding activity. A male bear searches for a female that will accept him. Lactating females do not breed, which means a female with cubs won't be interested. For this reason, a male may try to kill the cubs to bring the sow into heat. A black bear is sexually mature at about 3½ years old and it may breed for the first time that year or the year after.

Gestation is about 220 days. Females give birth in a den in late January or early February. Cubs of a 300-pound (135 kg) female weigh approximately 12 ounces (340 g) at birth. Most often, a sow gives birth to two cubs, but the litter count may vary from one to six young, depending on nutrition, food production and the age of the sow. Cubs generally remain with the sow for slightly longer than a year and disperse as yearlings.

Adult bears may weigh between 175 and 600 pounds (78 to 270 kg), depending on diet and genetics. In a study conducted in California's Tulare County, the average weight of adult male black bears was about 250 pounds (112 kg). The California Fish and Game Commission record for a black bear killed by a hunter is 574 pounds (258 kg).

Most black bears don't live much beyond the age of 25 years. In the wild, the average bear dies around the age of 18.

## Subspecies and Pelage

Black bears are easy to distinguish from brown (or grizzly) bears, but only after you've studied the differences. First of all, color is not a reliable indicator. A black bear can come in any shade, from almost white to black, while a brown bear may be blond to nearly black. Sometimes a brown bear has silver-tipped guard hairs that give it a grizzled look.

Three physical features distinguish brown bears from black bears. Brown bears have a dished-in face and a large hump above the shoulders. A brown bear's claws may measure up to 4 inches (10 cm) long. A black bear has a straight facial profile. It lacks the hump of the brown bear and it has shorter claws, approximately 1½ inches (3.8 cm) long. Many black bears have a patch of white hair on their chests.

Biologists currently recognize sixteen subspecies of black bear. From central British Columbia, through northern California, west of the Cascade Mountains and inland to the tip of northern Idaho, you'll find *Ursus americanus altifrontalis,* commonly referred to as the Olympic bear. *Ursus americanus californiensis* inhabits the central valley of California and into southern Oregon. The Idaho black bear or cinnamon bear, *Ursus americanus cinnamonum,* lives east of the Cascades.

Continuing north up the Pacific coast you'll find a white or cream-colored phase, *Ursus americanus kermodei,* on and around Kermode Island on the central coast of British Columbia. The bears of Vancouver Island are *Ursus americanus vancouveri. Ursus americanus carlottae* are found in the Queen Charlotte Islands and Alaska.

In Alaska, are three subspecies of black bear, which include *Ursus americanus perniger, Ursus americanus pugnax* and *Ursus americanus emmonsii.* The blue or glacier phase can be found in the Yakutat area and other parts of southeast Alaska. On the islands of southeast Alaska, only the black phase is in evidence.

Jim Morrell with a "hybrid" black/grizzly boar that he tagged while hunting in British Columbia. Bears with mixed blood are rare, but not unheard of.

# JUDGING BEAR—WHAT IS IT? HOW BIG IS IT?

Spring bear are difficult to judge. Take the time to look each one over. This one's ears are on the top of his head and appear larger in relation to the size of his skull. Also note how the legs appear rangy and the front legs have been rubbed. Only a long stalk or high-power optics will reveal these things to the hunter. Save your time and boot leather by using the best optics you can afford on a spring bear hunt.

**B**ear are, perhaps, the most difficult animals to judge. Once I hunted with a friend in eastern Oregon. We spotted a bear that, from our vantage point above the animal, appeared very small. "How big is it," Tod Lum asked.

I squinted through the binoculars. A young bear, I thought to myself. I would have guessed it in the 150-pound (67.5 kg) range. Possibly, a two-year-old. To Tod, I said it was big enough. Tod shot the bear. When we found it, I could see I was wrong. This was an average full-grown boar. Conversely, the bear that my daughter had killed that very morning looked very big when we first spotted it. But at the end of the day, when two bears were hanging in the barn, we could see very little difference between them.

Keep the time of the year in mind when evaluating bears at long range. Early in the year, if you see two bears together, you are probably looking at a sow with a cub or a yearling. Bears breed in June or July, so if you see two bears together at this time of year, it is potentially a boar and a sow, a breeding pair. In the fall, if you see a bear with a smaller bear, it is a female with a cub. At this time of year, the cub may weigh between 30 (13.5 kg) and 75 pounds (34 kg), while the sow may weigh between 200 (90 kg) and 250 pounds (112.5 kg).

Lone bears are toughest to judge. Here are some clues.

First, look at the head. Imagine a triangle between a bear's nose and ears. The point of the triangle is the tip of the nose and the base is between the ears. If the sides of the triangle are longer than the base between the ears, it is either a young male or a female. On a bear with all three sides of the triangle equal in length, you're looking at a big trophy male. Also look at the relative size of the ears. Small ears and a large head usually mean a large bear. A bear with ears that appear large and legs that appear long is a younger bear.

Next, look at the front feet. If they look big, it could be a male. Even younger males have bigger front feet.

Finally, if you can spot sex organs, you can dispel doubt as to whether you're looking at a male or a female. On a boar standing broadside, the penis sheath may be visible extending from the body just in front of the hind legs. You'll see this best when the bear is walking. From the rear, look for testicles. Females have a pointed patch of hair angling down and outward from the vulva. You'll see this drop of hair, often shiny with urine, a few inches (centimeters) below the tail.

When you go after a black bear, you might not take the first bear you find. It is illegal to hunt cubs or sows with cubs. If a trophy is desired, the game becomes even more difficult. The hunter needs to be more selective if looking for a bear rug. Later in the spring, many bears rub bare spots in their hides, scratching against boulders and trees. To qualify for record book entry, archery and blackpowder minimums are 18 inches (45.7 cm) for skull measurement, from front to back and side to side. Very few females qualify for the record book.

It might mean that you pass up the only bear you will see and never spot another. That's part of the challenge and why it's called hunting.

The claws of Retired Navy Commodore Jim Morrell's bear show marked grizzly characteristics, but exhibit the coloration of black bear claws.

Author Gary Lewis with a brown-phase black bear (above). This boar was feeding on apples, plums and berries near agricultural land. On this hunt, the fresh tracks of multiple bears were found before this bear was spotted across the river.

In the spring, as mating season approaches, a boar will often try to kill a sow's cubs in order to bring her into heat. Note the color difference in this pair of littermates (right).

The subspecies with the largest range is *Ursus americanus americanus,* which inhabits eastern Montana to the Atlantic and south to Texas. The bears of the island of Newfoundland are *Ursus americanus hamiltoni. Ursus americanus amblyceps* can be found in the American southwest and northern Mexico, while *Ursus americanus luteolus* inhabits eastern Texas, Louisiana and Mississippi. In north central Mexico is *Ursus americanus machetes. Ursus americanus eremicus* is found in northeastern Mexico and *Ursus americanus floridanus* lives in Florida, Georgia and Alabama.

Color phases of black bears vary greatly, even within a region. Among Olympic bears, black pelage is most common. Sightings in Oregon led observers to note that black bears outnumbered other color phases four to one. In one study in Oregon's Wallowa County, east of the Cascade Mountains, 46 percent of black bears had brown coats, 26 percent wore black coats, 24 percent were blondes and 4 percent were cinnamon. In Alaska, black-coated bears are most common, but cinnamon bears are seen in south central Alaska and the southeast mainland.

# BEATING A BEAR'S SENSES

To successfully hunt bear where they eat, sleep and procreate, you must beat the senses they employ to protect themselves. Every day, a bear relies upon his eyes, ears and nose to alert him to danger. He is far better at staying alive than we are at turning him into sausage.

Most hunters know that it is better to see the animal before it sees us. In fact, if such a thing were possible, we would find out that far more bear see us than we are aware of. How then do we beat his vision and see him first? The key lies in understanding how bear see.

## Sight

It was once believed that black bears see only in shades of gray and that a bear's eyes were rather poor. But today, scientists believe that bears can see rather well—perhaps as well as humans, at least at short range.

Bears are nearsighted, but tests have shown that black bears have color vision and are especially sensitive to the hues of blue and green. Being able to distinguish color is helpful for finding colored fruits and berries. Their binocular vision provides good depth perception. Bears also have good night vision, due to a reflective layer at the back of the eye called the tarpetum lucidum, which reflects light, allowing a second stimulus of the rods.

It is true that black bears rely less on sight and more on smell and sound to alert them to danger. But a black bear can see and focus on objects hundreds of yards away. His eye is tuned to pick up movement and discern pattern. If the bear is alerted by some scent drifting on the breeze or by a branch you just broke, he'll have his head up and he'll be looking around. It doesn't matter how much camouflage you're wearing, if you're moving in his field of vision, he's going to spot you.

Minimize your movement and you'll maximize the chances of seeing the bear before he sees you. To do this, your best bet is to identify the food source, find fresh tracks to confirm a bear is in the area and find a place to sit and watch, perhaps at the intersection of two trails or over a clearcut.

Camo clothing is helpful. Pick a pattern that blends into the natural surroundings where you hunt. Before you buy, look at the pattern from a distance. Does it all blend together when viewed from afar, or does it appear random and broken? You want a pattern that appears broken and doesn't go all black, all green or all brown when viewed from 50 yards (45.5 m) away.

For safety reasons, I believe that a hunter should wear high visibility hunter orange when hunting during firearm seasons. But the rifle hunter has options that will make him or her less visible to game. A hunter orange hat is a good compromise that a lot of hunters make for safety. A checkered shirt or jacket can provide the broken pattern that will keep you from standing out to the eyes of a bear.

Since a bear's vision is tuned to pick up action, keep the motion of your hands to a minimum. Don't wear hunter orange on your arms, hands, or legs. Your extremities are subject to the most movement. Don't dress them up in flashy color. Reduce the shine of your face by using face paint, a mask or a beard. In warm weather, wear mosquito net gloves to keep your hands from betraying you. In a bear's core area, when you move, move slowly.

Author Lee Van Tassell with bear taken in Oregon coast range, displaying the shoulder mass typical of a large boar.

Richard Baltz scans a clearcut across a canyon looking for that telltale black spot against a field of green. Scouting can tell the hunter if bears are in the area. Take the time to glass openings carefully. An hour or more spent glassing one area can pay off.

## Sound

I have hunted with people who make a lot of noise in bear country. Some people are just heavy walkers. I have hunted with others who make very little noise, moving as quietly as a light breeze. The quiet ones kill more bears.

Black bears hear far better than humans, thanks to ear construction that consists of a ball-shaped resonating chamber around the eardrum. Bears pay attention to anything that sounds foreign to their ears. If they learn to associate the sound of an approaching vehicle or a slammed door with two-legged predators, they'll be forewarned. When hunting bear, pay close attention to all the sounds you make.

Begin with the drive into the hunt area. Turn off the music and don't race the engine. When you park, set the emergency brake quietly. Don't slam the doors, the trunk, or the tailgate. Push them closed and lean against them until they click shut.

Wear boots or sneaking shoes that allow you to feel the branches beneath your feet. One successful bowhunter I know hunts only in his socks. Pick your way around downed branches instead of trying to walk through them. Be conscious of the sound of your footsteps. Be quiet. In dry weather, it is better to stay out of some areas until first light, just because it is hard to move without making noise.

Remember, if you startle one animal, even if it is a non-target animal, its attitude or body language may warn your prey that danger is near, and you probably won't get your opportunity.

Sounds can also alert you to bears. A feeding bear may paw through a rotten stump, roll over a log, dig out a ground squirrel, strip the bark from a tree or pull down a young deer. Key on that sound and you might surprise a bear in the middle of his meal.

Cubs often make a lot of racket when they play. A boar and a sow are not the quietest of lovers.

Lee Van Tassell was hunting with his brother Matt, when they located this bear by the sounds it made while feeding. Breaking limbs and splashing gave this bear away.

The fewer sounds you make and the more time you sit and listen, the better your chances.

Bears are generally quiet, but they make a number of sounds that are easily recognized. Growls are distinctive and are used as a warning to keep humans and other predators (including bears) away. A bear may grunt when it is surprised or injumore than any other sense. The sniff may be followed by a grunt or a growl.

While feeding, the bear may make very little noise, but it can make quite a commotion in a stand of young trees as it strips bark or bites off the young buds. The bear may turn over a stump or roll rocks to find grubs or ants. He might paw through a rotten log.

The successful bear hunter listens as much as he looks and is alert to every sound that might give away a bear's location. The undergrowth may conceal the bear for a period of time, but eventually the bear will move out into an opening.

A woof is used to alert other bears, to warn an intruder, and call to cubs. It is not uncommon to hear a whimper or a moan from a bear that is cornered or treed. A dying bear may make a "death moan," a long series of bawls that trails out at the end.

On a hunt in Alaska, I stalked a bear in thick brush on a steep hillside. As I closed to within 50 yards (45.5 m), I lost sight of it, but it knew I was coming. First, I heard a moan and then the big boar began to clack his teeth at me. I backed off. That bear could have his hill.

Black bears are nothing if not unpredictable. And it is tricky to predict one bear's behavior based on the behavior of other bears. Each is an individual and is different from every other. If a bear clacks or pops its teeth, it is annoyed or alarmed. This is a warning of a "bluff" or a charge and is a very real threat.

Author Gary Lewis tests the wind with a squeeze bottle filled with powder. A bear's nose is its most trusted asset and a hunter has to beat the wind to put a tag on a black bear.

## Smell

From time to time a bear may see you and mistake you for some other creature. He may hear you breaking limbs and think a herd of elk is moving through. But he never makes a mistake with his nose.

A bear uses his nose to find food, locate mates, avoid danger and identify cubs. It is thought that a bear's nose is seven times better than a bloodhound's. The area of nasal mucous membrane in a bear's head is one hundred times larger than a human's. In the roof of the mouth, a bear has an organ called a Jacobson's organ, which also improves the sense of smell.

According to The Great Bear Almanac by Gary Brown, a black bear in California was seen to travel upwind 3 miles (4.8 km) in a straight line to reach the carcass of a dead deer. A male polar bear has been seen to travel up to 40 miles (64 km) to reach a prey animal he detected on the wind. And a black bear was able to detect a human scent more than fourteen hours after the person passed along the trail. A male can also detect which way a breeding female is traveling just by sniffing her tracks.

Bears use their extraordinary olfactory ability to communicate with each other. Scent is left on trees and vegetation to let other bears know they are nearby.

On the hunt, wind can be your ally or your biggest enemy. Your scent is frightening to most animals. It signals danger. A bear's ability to smell is the one sense that they never question. The better you understand how bear react to dangerous odors, the better you will be able to exploit their sense of smell.

If the wind is steady from one direction, hunt into it. A steady wind is the friend of the still-hunter. I carry and use a product called Little Smokey, a white powder in a squeeze bottle. Squirted in the air, it allows me to read wind direction at a glance. I rely on it, checking the wind constantly to make sure that the animal I am hunting won't catch my scent.

One time my friend Dave Hamilton was bow-hunting elk in eastern Oregon when he smelled a rotten carcass and followed it in. As he moved in closer, he could hear a bear feeding on what turned out to be a dead five-point bull. The smell was overpowering, Dave said, but the bear was cautious, even as it fed inside the elk's cavity. Repeatedly it raised its nose to scent-check the wind and look around. A bear's nose is so well-developed that it can even smell while it is around a rotten elk.

Dave had a bear tag in his pocket and an arrow on the string. Stalking the predator from behind, he waited until the bear's vitals were exposed and shot the bruin from 10 yards (9.1 m). Dave's approach, coming in straight downwind into the smell of the carcass is what allowed him to get so close. With the animal distracted, he'd beat its sense of sight and its hearing. Don't ever fool yourself into believing that a bear might not smell you. If the wind is at your back the bear knows you're there and you have severely limited your chance of success.

When scouting or hunting, watch where you walk and what you brush up against. Your scent will transfer to the brush, leaving a faint, lingering smell that warns animals of your presence long after you are gone. One habit that many hunters have is to pull a twig with their fingers, idly playing with it while they walk, eventually discarding it and pulling another twig. If you indulge in this, you are advertising your presence.

Scent control is just as important to the tree stand hunter. When you choose your stand locations, pick a spot to take advantage of the prevailing wind and pick an alternate for those days when the wind is coming from the other direction. If the wind appears to be swirling, it is better to back out of the hunt area and try another tactic rather than risk blowing a well-scouted location by spooking the animals out of it.

There are times when you can use your scent to advantage. When you hunt a bed or feeding area, your scent can act as a driver, and push a bear out ahead of you toward a hunter on stand. This tactic has accounted for a good many bears over the years.

This bear's posture indicates he's relying on his nose more than his eyesight. A curious, hungry or alerted bear may stand on hind legs to get his nose in the upper air currents.

## RANGE AND COVER

At one time, the black bear's range stretched across most of North America to include all of Canada and much of Mexico. Today the range is fragmented, with bears found in remaining forest zones across the U.S., Canada and Mexico. In some southern and eastern states, bear numbers are low to non-existent.

Perhaps 40 percent of the black bears in the United States live in Alaska. Other states with large populations of black bears include Washington, Oregon, Idaho, California, Montana, Wyoming, Maine and Minnesota. In Canada, British Columbia, Ontario and Quebec hold most of the black bears, thanks to the quality of the forest habitat.

Black bears seek out country that makes for easy living in every season of the year. They find it most often in forestland where the ground is moist. Shade and water are important factors that bears rely on all year long. While bears are primarily forest dwellers, you may also find them working along a beach at sea level, dining on morsels brought in on the tide, or above timberline in the summer, foraging on berries.

Cub survival is directly linked to the presence of trees for escape. During the warmest months, shade is important for temperature regulation. For bedding, bears also prefer heavy cover near feeding areas and will hollow out a depression sheltered from extreme weather and wind. Stumps and logs are also an important factor for winter sleep and the birthing and rearing of cubs.

When scouting for bears, focus on moisture-laden ground with dark timber for shade, especially in the early fall hunt (above).

Abundant rain, lush green growth, dark timber and a steady supply of Sitka blacktail deer and salmon makes this island prime coastal black bear country (left).

Old clearcuts containing water, berries, immature trees and rotten logs draw bears from the nearby dark timber and shorelines (far left).

## Dens

In northern latitudes, black bears are long-winter snoozers and may spend up to seven months in their den. To the south, however, winter sleep may be full-time or intermittent, depending on climate and food availability.

The primary purpose of the den is to serve as shelter during the winter, when forage is difficult to reach. Dens are chosen to help the bear conserve body heat. In the winter, the warmer the bear can stay, the less precious fat is burned. Because cubs are born in the winter, the den serves as a secure birthing site where the sow can nourish the cubs in safety.

Pregnant females are most likely to either use cavities or excavate. Dens of other bears, especially in areas with mild and snowless winters, may consist of grasses and leaves shaped into nest-like structures on the surface of the ground, perhaps in dense habitat against the trunk of a tree or under a brush pile. Rock outcroppings, caves, hollow logs, trees, stumps, eagle nests and excavated holes in the ground are also potential den sites. Bears may also choose humanmade housing. Cabins, woodsheds and drainage culverts have been used.

Studies in Idaho found that bears in that state preferred hollow trees with a diameter of 44 to 75 inches (1.1 to 1.9 m). A 1987 study in Alaska gave a minimum of 39 inches (0.98 m) in diameter. A 1976 study found that bears preferred trees with an average 64-inch (1.6 m) diameter. In an Oregon study, bears were located in trees, stumps and downed logs with an average 55 inches (1.4 m) in diameter.

## Use of Roads and Trails

Studies have shown that roads and trails in and through bear habitat do not negatively affect bears. Hunters often find bear scat and tracks going right down the center of a road. In some habitats, whe`re grass grows along the roadbed, bears feed on the shoulder.

Human use of roads, however, does have an impact on bears. Roads bring conflict with vehicles and roads bring hunters. Road closures limit human activity. The smart hunter pays attention. In forest ground, wherever you find roads that have been gated and locked against vehicle use, you will find the trail of a black bear.

A dugout entrance that opened into a 6-foot-diameter (1.8 m), deep, cool cave in the muskeg.

Ground dens may be used in the summer time as well as in the winter.

The second bear of the day responded to the call in 15 minutes. Above, Tod Lum shows off his prize, a September bear, summer-fat on hawthorn berries, apples and plums (above).

A well-used trail in the muskeg (top right). This could be a great place to set up a trail camera. Bear are creatures of habit. The trails they walked last year are the trails they'll take this year.

Rotting timber (bottom right) is laden with larva that provides much-needed protein in the summer and fall.

## SEASONAL BEHAVIOR

We think in terms of four seasons: winter, spring, summer and fall. It is easy to simplify and generalize about where you might find a bear, but food sources change weekly. Fall, for instance, can be separated into many smaller intervals. Blueberries, huckleberries, blackberries, salmonberries, pears, plums, and apples ripen at different times. The bears in any given area learned as cubs to move from one food source to another. They follow a similar path each autumn, feasting on nature's bounty as it comes into season.

A bear's home range may cover anywhere from one to 60 square miles (156 sq km), dependent on availability of feed, elevation and status in the pecking order. A bear's travels revolve around his food sources, and these change on a weekly basis. Think in terms of specific foods at specific intervals in the season.

Start with a map of a drainage or mountain range. It should show enough detail that you can identify terrain features. Mark each bear sighting on your map, along with the date and the apparent food source. Fresh scat can tell you what the bears are eating.

Don't think in terms of generalities about bears in the region. Instead, concentrate on the food sources in a particular watershed. Focus on what the dominant bear in the area might be eating. Then make a list of the foods on the menu and determine the order in which they are available. As the season progresses, move from food source to food source. You'll find the trails leading from feed to bedding cover to water.

At fence lines, look for long black hairs stuck in the barbed wire. Watch for tracks down by the creek. In heavy cover, black bears may use logging roads to move from one place to another. On closed or seldom-used roads you'll find their tracks going right down the center of the road. But remember, black bears feed primarily during the daytime, especially when not disturbed by humans, but they normally wait until close to dark to enter large clearings.

Follow the feed and you'll be on the right trail. But before you find the bears, you might find some other creatures. Raccoons, those ringed-tail bandits, are intelligent, inquisitive, adaptable and excellent climbers—just like bears. They eat fish, crustaceans, insects, smaller mammals, fruit, berries and corn—just like bears. If easy food is available on your back porch or in a barn or outbuilding, raccoons will find it—just like bears.

On the hunt, whether in a Western berry patch or over a bait barrel in a Minnesota swamp, a visit from a raccoon may foreshadow the approach of a bruin. Raccoons keep different schedules than bears to stay out of the way of the larger predators. And the little varmints will most certainly be on the watch as they browse on berries or raid the bait. If the raccoons suddenly head for cover, a bear may be on the way in.

## Spring

In most western states and provinces, spring bear hunting is controlled by a lottery system. Interested hunters need apply early because the tags are allotted before other big-game tags. It's a great time to be in the high country in April when the western anenome and Cusick's paintbrush is in bloom. In May you can expect Canby's lovage and not long after that yellow columbine, mountain buttercup and fireweed. You'll probably see some elk and maybe a few turkeys. The deer will be shedding their gray winter coats for the red-brown of summer and the bears will be feeding on the high grassy slopes.

From early spring until the middle of May, bears are focused on food. And the more you follow the feed from the first green-up in the valleys to the bloom of wildflowers on the mountain slopes, the more often you'll find bears. Each week of the season, the food sources change. The skunk cabbage blooms in late March and April and then the grasses grow, fiddleheads appear on the ferns, bulbs sprout new shoots and aspens begin to bud. In the rivers, carp or trout may move in close to the bank on spawning runs. Bears may feed on fish at this time of year as well. Anticipate the food sources as bear key on each new menu item.

In spring, with the main focus on food, bears are acutely aware of any new sources. Traveling to find food is something these bruins are very good at doing.

# THE SPRING HUNT

Timbered valleys split the grassy slopes into long green fingers stretching down toward the river. Matt Smith lifted the ten-power binoculars to his eyes. A gust of wind blew his blond hair back and he could smell the wildflowers on the warm breeze.

For weeks he'd been searching these slopes for a legal bear. Now, with only a day before the end of the spring bear season, warmer weather had the wildflowers in bloom and the elk out of the river bottoms in search of food.

Moving to a different vantage point, he sat, put the glasses to his eyes and immediately saw a bear, feeding along the bottom of the drainage.

The bear Matt spotted was a blond. Checking the wind, Matt stood up and glanced back at his partner. Jeremy could see five bears on the opposite slope, one of which was a sow they had spotted earlier in the season. She had black legs, a blond body and a red head. With her were two cinnamon colored cubs and one black cub. The fifth bear was a big blond boar with black legs. Matt's bear was within 800 yards (728 m) and the other bears were about a mile and a half away.

Moving on a course to intersect with the path the first bear was taking, Matt couldn't find it when he reached the bottom of the slope. From where he sat he could see occasional glimpses of the big boar as he made his way through the timber downhill and for almost four hours he watched the sow and cubs. Laying on her back, the old lady picked up rocks in her paws and shook them to catch the grubs and worms beneath. The cubs were running and playing all around her and should they get too close she'd swat them down the hill.

He was about to head back when he saw the first bear again, just below him, 200 yards (182 m) away, flipping rocks over and prospecting for grubs. Lying down, Matt settled the rifle into his shoulder and found the bear in his crosshairs.

Author Lee Van Tassell tagged this big boar after glassing steep, clearcut slopes. His 45 minutes of glassing this particular slope paid off when this boar followed a sow out of the timber.

## Spring Food Sources

Spring bear hunts begin in April and run through May and June. The bears are emerging from winter dens at this time and are feeding primarily on grass, bugs and grubs to get their digestive juices flowing again. A black bear's preferred menu includes just about anything edible. In the spring, grasses figure heavily in their diet as they regenerate digestive juices.

Depending on the region, a bear might eat a variety of grasses, herbs and forbs, including wild onion, sarsaparilla, rhubarb, lupine, northern bedstraw, lousewort, Labrador tea, and coffeeberry. And where you find wild strawberries, keep an eye out for bear. Tree cambium, dogwood, manzanita and kinnikinnick are also favored foods.

Early in the spring, bears often select open hillsides or meadows to take advantage of the fresh grass. As the weather warms and more food becomes available, a black bear may change elevation to utilize another resource.

On the Pacific coast, by the fourth week of spring, the bear's appetite is whetted for something to supplement his diet of grass. By this time, the sap is running in the hemlock trees. Bears peel the bark off the tree to get at the cambium layer, often killing the tree in the process. Later in the spring, the sap is running in cedar, fir trees, white pine, alder and spruce. For a change of taste, the bears move out of the hemlocks and attack new stands of trees.

Later, as the snows recede, they'll uncover winter-killed deer and elk, which are a bonus. And a bear may also dig out ground squirrels or catch deer fawns or elk calves in the spring and summer. When deer fawns, elk calves and moose calves are born; bears may change their diets again, preying on the helpless young.

Swampy drainages, containing skunk cabbage (above) will draw and hold bears from spring through fall.

Fiddleheads (left), the new growth on ferns, are an indicator that other foods that bears like should be in abundance in the area.

## Spring Travel Patterns

As the foliage in the river bottoms dries out, the bears climb higher in search of succulent grass. This brings them out into the open on green sun-lit slopes where they graze for hours, eating grass and turning over rocks in their search for grubs.

Usually, when you spot a bear on the spring slopes, it is on the other side of a canyon. This is not easy hunting. The bruin may be a mile (1.6 km) or more away when first seen so the hunter will have to move in close for a good shot to be taken. That means within 200 yards (182 m) for a rifle and less than 30 (27.3 m) for a good shot with a bow. It probably means crossing a creek or river at the bottom and it may take hours to reach the spot where the bear was first seen. That bear could be long gone by the time you get there. Constantly moving while he feeds, a big boar can cover a lot of ground in a hurry, though if unmolested, it will probably stay in the same general area all day.

In coastal habitat, spring bear hunting is often pursued in a different fashion. Because of the dense cover, spot and stalk tactics are more difficult. So, many hunters walk mountain roads in the early evening to take up a stand downwind of a clearcut or a meadow, watching and waiting until a bear is spotted. Ask questions and scout first to find an area being used by bears.

Look first for good habitat providing access to denning areas, water, succulent plants and other springtime food sources. Once you have picked an area meeting all these criteria then spend time there, searching for sign.

Learn to spot a bear's tracks. In forests with thick cover, a black bear travels established trails and old logging roads. You can often find the tracks they leave on these roads. An intimate knowledge of your hunting area helps you determine where that bear was feeding and give an indication of where you might find him again.

Black bear droppings may sometimes be shaped like an apple fritter. Though not quite as tasty, they contain hints at where to find the bear. The color of fresh droppings may reveal that a bear

was eating grass, robbing an ant hill or finding grubs in rotten logs and stumps. These clues can lead you to a feeding area.

In late-May and June, adult bears move into the mating season. And, while they still must eat, they turn part of their focus to breeding impulses. Now is the time to target the core areas where you found the most sign in the early season. Watch open meadows or clearcuts for hours at a time. This is the time of year when patience and scouting can pay off with multiple bear sightings and stalk opportunities.

At this time of the season, pay special attention to road closure areas as decreased human access will mean a better chance of finding the animal you are looking for.

Dry soil gives greater definition to this obviously fresh bear print (top).

A massive paw print in an Alaskan muskeg with a .30-06 round shown for scale. Sometimes, one boar will control an area. His tracks can give him away and show the path he takes to feed and bed (above).

## Fall

In September, the days begin to grow shorter and the leaves turn yellow on the trees. Nights are colder and the lazy days of summer are gone. To make it through the winter, a bear needs to bulk up, to pack on the fat that will sustain it for several months in hibernation. Fall patterns are dependent on the food sources. These change quickly in September and October. They also change from year to year, dependent on the production of berries, fruit and acorns. Fish runs and big game populations also play a part in a bear's autumn ramblings.

My wife once sat against a tree in an apple orchard and waited for a blacktail buck. What showed up instead was a small bear. In the creek bottom, it was out of sight but she could hear it crashing in the brush in the blackberry bushes. Merrilee had no bear tag or desire to take a bear. I showed up fifteen minutes too late and found its tracks along the creek. We traced its footprints with our fingertips. The bear had been less than twenty yards from her.

To find a bear in the fall, hunt the food sources that are available. In September, hunt the high mountain meadows and the old burns where huckleberries grow. On high, alpine mountains, small berry bushes such as crowberry, blueberry and bear berry are a food source for a bruin. One year there may be berries everywhere, another year a late spring frost can kill most berries. Where blackberries grow wild, a hunter can find a bear by watching the trails where he finds tracks. Patience pays for the bear hunter.

Apples (left) are a favored fall food when bears can get them. Gaining access to agricultural land can tip the balance in favor of the hunter.

During years of good berry production (below), bears may travel for miles to gorge while the fruit lasts. When the supply dries up, they move on in search of other food sources.

# THE FALL HUNT

Later in the year, a bear needs to make meat. When the berries are gone and the fruit is off the trees, bear begin to key on big game. And anything could be on the menu. Knowing this, I kept a bear tag in my pocket when I hunted for elk.

Dark clouds rolled overhead and a cold wind blew scattered snowflakes in my face as I moved quietly down through the timber. There were patches of snow on the ground and the promise of much more to come. It was mid-November, elk season, and my chances for tagging an elk were lessening as my time in the woods was drawing to a close. Still-hunting, I'd take a few steps, pause and look carefully in all directions before moving again. It was close to five o'clock. There was little more than an hour of daylight left.

I glimpsed movement through the trees, a flash of black or brown. I swung up the binoculars for a closer look. A bear. He moved with a rolling gait, his summer fat rolling beneath a shiny fall coat.

He was quartering away at 200 yards (182 m), visible only for a few seconds. I passed up the shot and sat down against a tree where I had good visibility in all directions except for immediately behind me. If I could call the bear in before

nightfall I'd be able to take a higher percentage shot and lay the bear beside the coyote I'd taken earlier in the day. If I had to quit calling because it was too dark to shoot then I'd be walking back to camp in the dark with a salivating bear nearby, not to mention any other hungry sharp-toothed critters that might have been drawn in by my predator call.

The shadows were lengthening and I never felt so alive as I pondered the possibilities of luring a black bear in to his dinner, which could quite easily turn out to be me. I called at a constant rate for 45 minutes, pausing only to catch my breath. I imagined the bear circling to try to catch a scent, but I never saw him. And the shadows lengthened.

Away down the hill I heard the growl of an engine, a pickup truck coming slowly along the road in low gear. It came into sight and I hoped he would turn right at the fork and go along elsewhere but he turned left on the road above me. Tracking the bear later, I found it had circled me as I called it, pausing to look down into the canyon to where I had been. For 45 minutes it had never been more than 400 yards (364 km) from me. The hunters in the truck, coming along the road when they did, spooked it.

## Fall Food Sources

In the fall, fruits and mast (nuts and fruits on the ground) are staples, but bears also feed on carrion and insects, such as yellow jackets, bees (and honey), termites and carpenter ants. Bears search rotten stumps and logs for grubs. On occasion, they find a beehive. I once came upon a bear in early September near the headwaters of the Willamette. It was pawing through a log and the bees were swarming about its head. I was less than thirty yards away, with an arrow on the string, when it caught my scent and bolted.

The bees went after it. I waited until they were all gone and took a look. There was a honeycomb, half-eaten, inside.

Where you find oak trees, beeches, hickories and hazel trees, you may also find bear tracks, as bear feed on the mast. They return year after year to hardwood forests when acorns carpet the ground beneath the oak trees.

As the berries ripen in the summer and early fall, the bears will seek out these crops, sometimes feeding with reckless abandon on blueberry, cranberry, huckleberry, blackberry, gooseberry, hawthorn berry and raspberry. Rose hips, squawroot, dandelion, clover and thistle are also favored foods.

In the summer and early fall, bears may enter orchards to feed on apples, cherries, pears and plums as these fruits ripen and fall to the ground. But hungry bears may also climb the tree and rest among the branches while they dine. A downwind stand taken in a nearby tree can yield the hunter a bruin.

Likewise, black walnut, buffaloberry, lomatium, cowparsnip, pine nuts, chestnut and chinkapin mast are targeted in season. Pawpaw, persimmons, sassafras and elderberry are also on the menu.

If there are fish running in nearby streams, bears prowl the banks in the hopes of catching salmon, suckers, steelhead or trout. They prefer to catch and eat live fish, but, as the season progresses, they settle for spawned-out fish. In the south, some bears have learned to dine on alligator eggs to their peril.

In late September through October, salmon can be found in many coastal waters. As the fish climb higher on their spawning runs they become vulnerable to bears. After they have spawned they die and their bodies are washed up on gravel bars. An alert hunter, on stand or moving stealthily into the wind, can often surprise a bear fishing for his dinner.

In areas with large salmon runs, bears move to the river bottoms and prowl the sandbars. When fresh fish are in the stream, most bears ignore rotting carcasses for a chance to grab a prime salmon. At this time, a dominant bear stakes out a section of stream. Other bears may enter his domain, but only for a quick dash and grab, and a return to safety.

In October and November when berry season has passed and bears are searching for meat, calling can produce a bear. Sporting goods stores now have a wide array of calls that a bear hunter can use. Rabbit in distress calls can be employed, as can fawn and calf calls. Several companies offer bear calls that imitate the squall of a cub. Bears can and will come in to elk bugling.

At higher elevations (left), bears find cool air in summer and early fall. They also find patches of berries and nuts on which to feed. At this time of year, they feed opportunistically and may come readily to a call.

Close examination of fresh scat (below) offers a clue to the food source and where to find the bear.

Jennifer Lewis (bottom) walks down the hill back to camp at the end of a fall morning's hunt.

## Late Fall Feeding Binge

It is a simple principle. A skinny bear in November will be a dead bear by May. Hibernation may last almost seven months. A bear will lose up to thirty percent of its weight in the process. If it doesn't pack on the lard in the last few weeks before the long sleep, it will starve to death in its den.

When the weather turns cool and the nights are getting long, the bear instinctively knows it's running out of time. Boars and sows throw caution to the wind and go on a serious feeding binge.

The bruin must put on a thick layer of fat. For the next six months or so, the fat serves as a reserve of nutrition and water and as a blanket against the cold.

During the late fall feeding binge, going almost around the clock, a black bear will consume up to 20,000 calories a day and put on as much as 30 pounds (13.5 kg) in a week. He naps for short periods of time and, if food is scarce, will travel up to 100 miles (161 km) to hit a big supply of groceries. At this time, he is focused on the feed and is not prone to wander in the typical fashion of a summer bear. He'll put on the feed bag, eat night and day then turn around and head for home.

This is not a time to squander energy. Oil-rich nuts are a primary food, as are fruits and berries. Salmon too are rich in oils. Where a bear might have focused on eating only fresh fish in September, he will devour the rotting carcasses in November. Croplands too, are a target, even harvested crops like corn, where an animal can prospect for abundant leftovers.

In November, find the food source and hunt there, not where you found bears feeding on grubs or low-calorie grasses in the spring. Hunt the water sources too. Not only are the bears bingeing on food, they're far thirstier than usual. Find a rich food source and water and chances are good there'll be a bear nearby.

Knowing that bears will binge in the weeks before denning, scout the high-calorie food sources during the spring and early fall seasons, and while hunting other big game. Contact a wildlife biologist in the hunt area and find out when the adult males go into hibernation. You should plan the hunt for three weeks prior to denning time.

## Dynamics of Food Sources and Travel Patterns

The bear is an opportunist. Over the course of the year, he eats almost anything from a menu that includes a wide range of plants and animals. Some bears rely primarily on plant material and carrion, while other bears kill their food. Habitat, social issues and prey all have an influence on a bear's diet.

Studies have shown that acorns are a vital dietary item for bears. For example, when insects rendered acorns inedible in a California study area in 1980, three of four radio-monitored adult female black bears moved to areas where undamaged acorns were available.

Changes in the habitat affect the bears' habits in various ways. A fire or a timber harvest might spur substantial new growth, ensuring high food production for several years. In such places, bear populations have exploded as the carrying capacity of the land has increased.

As timber grows taller, new growth diminishes and bears shift to another area with more habitat diversity. Timber harvest practices such as shelterwood, partial cuts or select cuts that open dense canopies allow for an increase in type of plant species that provide food and leave trees for escape.

Early in the cycle of timber management, bears find more grasses, forbs and berry-producing plants. In later stages, bears focus on fungi, ants, insects, and grubs living in the dead and dying material on the forest floor.

In stands of timber, bears may peel tree bark to get at the cambium layer. Peeling usually takes place in the spring. Such activity has a significant economic impact on timber management companies. Potential losses of timber to bears can figure in the millions of dollars at harvest age. Evidence of peeling may be found anywhere, but certain bear populations are habituated to the practice. Peeling and girdling of trees has been found to be more significant in northwestern Washington than in other regions.

It is thought that peeling occurs when bears have few food sources early in the season. It is probably a learned behavior. In a 1990 study, Schmidt and Gourley posited that sows with cubs were most likely to peel trees. A Washington study indicated that younger bears, that had been unable to establish territories were to blame.

Bear numbers have declined in some regions in North America as development has taken its toll of wildlife habitat. But black bear populations are at all-time highs in many areas. On the east coast, hunting seasons have been instituted where they have been closed for years. It is legal to take bear in spring and fall seasons in many western states and provinces. Restrictions may have tightened in some locales, but the hunting has continued to improve. And in many places, it has never been better.

# CHAPTER TWO

# Planning A Bear Hunt

When it comes time to plan, the first question to ask is, "How do I want to hunt?" For a chase with dogs, the thrill is limited to states where hunting with hounds is legal. If your ideal bear hunt is in a tree stand over a bait station, perhaps a trip to Idaho, the upper Midwest, East Coast or Canada is in order. For spot-and-stalk action on public land, try any one of the western states.

One way to quickly learn which areas hold high concentrations of bears is to look over the big game regulations. Many states hold a statewide fall hunt, but the areas with the most bruins also hold a spring hunt to provide more opportunity for sportsmen. Find a region that offers an additional tag or an extended season that runs from August through November and you've found a place to hunt.

## GATHERING INFORMATION

Lay out a map of your chosen state. Look for the one or two or three best areas in the state for bear, then pick up the telephone. Call a wildlife biologist in the state office of the Fish and Wildlife department. Ask which areas have the highest concentrations of black bear. Circle these on your map. Next, ask for a local wildlife biologist contact in each region. These are the people who know what is happening. These are the people whose telephones ring when a bear raids a camp or kills a pig. If there are damage complaints, they're the ones keeping the list. In some regions, bear damage complaints come in six months out of the year. Time to zoom in a little closer.

Places where types of habitat overlap, such as in this swamp, offer good food and water for a bear fresh from his winter sleep.

County maps and Game Management Unit charts show roadways and streams and major terrain features, but you want better information. Here's where a Bureau of Land Management (BLM) map or Forest Service map or one of the state atlas books can really come in handy. BLM and Forest Service maps show ownership of the land and often come with rudimentary topographical information. The state atlas books have better topography, but little in the way of ownership. I use as many charts as I can get to plan a hunt. At this stage, it's nice to have a map with a scale of 1 inch = 1 mile (2.5 cm = 1.6 km).

Talk to the wildlife biologist contact at the local level. Listen for clues that he or she might give regarding specific mountain ranges and watersheds. Not only do you need a plan, you need a plan B, plan C and plan D. Once you've narrowed down your options to four solid locations, it's time to zoom in again with a topo map.

## Topographic Maps

Topography, as defined by Random House Dictionary, is "the art of describing on maps and charts the physical features of an area, as mountains and rivers." Now is not the time to skimp and try to save a few dollars. A hunter needs

detail and resolution and they are found on the 7.5 Minute Series, 1:24000 scale U.S. Geological Survey maps. These maps are also called quadrangles or quads and they are indispensable for pre-scouting, scouting and the hunt. In the field, I carry my maps in zipper-lock bags to keep them from falling apart due to moisture. When they get old, I transfer all my little pencil marks to a new one and start over again.

This is part of what I call pre-scouting. Lay the topographic, or topo, map out on the table. Orient the top of the map to the north. At the bottom of the map, there's a scale and a declination symbol which shows true north and magnetic north. A legend on the bottom right shows the symbols for primary highways, secondary highways, light duty roads and unimproved roads.

The map is sectioned by a red, dashed-line grid at one-mile intervals. All known terrain features are mapped and named. Barrow pits, meadows, old mines and camps are identified along with a host of other features. All waterways are shown in solid blue line. The ones that are intermittent show up as dashed lines. If a pack trail once was used to move gear from a parking area to a mine, chances are the path is marked on the chart.

It may take more than one topo to cover all of a bear's potential range. To locate a particular river canyon, follow the river downstream to the next map. The name of the next map is found by looking at the edge of the chart. At the boundary in parentheses is the name, which usually refers to some major terrain feature such as a mountain or a lake.

With a 1:24000 USGS topo, you can plan hunts in places that other hunters might have missed. The topo helps a hunter to find the hidden springs and ponds where game finds water in dry times and the places that are sheltered from the wind, where animals can take refuge in colder weather. With a good topo, it's easy to identify the south-facing slopes and the valleys where the snows melt first, uncovering the new grass and last winter's kills. With the scale and detail of these topos, it is easy to pinpoint the biggest roadless areas, identify swamps, scope out north-facing ridges and find most of the springs and even some of the seeps.

Good bear country is wet country and that often means north faces and moss and springs and tangles. And lower elevation is better in the springtime. These bottomland spots are also where the

skunk cabbage can start. In wet climates the grass is going to grow on the sunny south-facing slopes and in the three- to five-year-old clearcuts and creek bottom drainages with enough openings where sunlight can come in. In dry climates, the north face is generally better. Habitat that supports a beaver is also a good place to find a bruin.

In the clear cuts in early spring, it's all about the grasses. Find tall grasses on the clear cuts and closed logging roads that have grown over. Clover patches are gold mines this time of year. Find the food and find the bedding areas, then locate the trails that connect them.

Mountains and hill tops are marked with an "X" at the summit, next to a number which gives the elevation. Contour lines descend from the sum-

Topographical maps (above) and aerial photos show the drainages, swamps, saddles and ridgelines in bear territory. Some things just need to be seen in person, like bears in trees (left).

When scouting new coutnry, remember that bears do better away from human influences. Closed roads and rugged ground discourage the faint of heart, giving the bear hunter a chance to get away from the crowd.

mit and are given at 40-foot (12.2 m) intervals. If the lines are close together, that means the hill is steep. If the lines are further apart, it means the ground has little slope. The map may be colored in shades of green. Dark green means the soil is the wetter, in season. A white background signifies that there are few if any trees in the area. Pay attention to such places. These are the spots where you might find a bear track in early spring.

Not only are feeding areas readily identified, with a little interpretation, a hunter can also identify escape routes and make an estimate about where to find the dense cover where a wounded bear will go. Best of all, when you're hiking out with an empty gun and a full pack frame, you can find the route that leads to the nearest road with the least gain in elevation.

Remember, bears establish their home territories to make the best use of the terrain. Identify a basin or a valley or a river bottom in bear country and you're likely pinpointing the home of one or more bruins. From there, look at food availability in the surrounding area.

First, where is the bear likely to find grass in the first weeks of spring? Second, might the bear be peeling trees as the sap begins to run, or looking for prickly pears? Third, where would the bear be able to find deer fawns or elk calves? In early autumn the fruit will be ripening on the trees and on the berry bushes. Where would that bear go to find berries? By late fall, he'll be keying on elk herds again or prowling the river for spawning salmon. Know the food sources and you'll be close.

Remember, it's all about the groceries. The bear finds food in the swamp, along the logging roads, on the hillside slides and in the high meadows, depending on the time of year. Pinpoint the likely sources. Find them first with a topo map then refer to an aerial photo to get more of the story.

## Aerial Photos

Aerial photos are readily available these days thanks to Internet web sites (http://nationalmap.gov/gio/viewonline.html) and mapping companies (www.maptech.com and www.mytopo.com) that cater to hunters. Lay an aerial photo next to a topographical map and find the detail that other hunters miss. You'll find the tall timber and the roads that might not show up on the maps. If there's a pond on the map, the photo will show if there's any water in it.

Now look for places far from any road. Don't be like most hunters. Most hunters won't go more than 1/2 mile (0.8 km) from the road where they parked the truck. Many won't travel more than 300 yards (273 m) from the truck. And most hunters want to be out of the woods before dark. Most hunters never see a bear. They simply limit their chances of success because they haven't taken the time to learn to use map and compass and are afraid to get lost.

Study the map and aerial photo to determine likely feeding and travel routes. Try to pick out possible escape routes. Where would your bear bed? Probably up against a rock wall or under a fallen tree where there would be some shade in the afternoon if the weather is warm. Sometimes right out in the open on an early spring day. And it would have at least two escape routes. No wild animal wants to be trapped.

### Wildlife Biologists

Knowing how to find a bear's home territory on a map is important, so is a good conversation with the local wildlife biologist. These people know where the bears are. They also know why they are there. I have learned more talking to a biologist for a half-hour than I used to learn in a whole season on my own.

The key is in asking the right questions. These are public servants. They are there to serve the public good and the good of the wildlife. In most cases, they are hunters themselves. Treat them with the respect their education and experiences deserve.

Ask about the previous year's winter-kill. Ask about deer fawn and elk calf recruitment. Ask what corners of the units they manage are the most productive. After asking, shut up and let them talk. There is no need to impress them. Be friendly and thank them for their time. These men and women can be a valuable resource.

If access is difficult to a particular area, find out if there is a better way in. Perhaps they have a contact with a landowner who has complained about bear damage in the past. They usually keep a record of such people and might fax with a list of phone numbers

Finally, the maps and aerial photos reveal the access points and the best trails through the area. How the hunt area is accessed is vital to bear hunting success.

## ACCESS

When the hunt area is impossible to reach by car or truck, it may be reached by boot leather or by bicycle. On one state-line hunt, we used a boat. We crossed the bridge at the border, drove a couple of dozen miles downstream and launched to access the public land that was locked up by private ground and the river.

Dan Turner jumped out of the boat and pulled it up on the rocky beach. We clambered out, hauling our packs and rifles away from the water. I looked up the rocky canyon and wondered what the next three days held in store.

In Alaska, skiffs and inflatables are used to reach into tidal pools where larger boats can't access and bears like to feed.

The hunters used a boat to access this canyon on a spring bear hunt. Spike camp was made on an overlook to take advantage of the view of the opposite slope.

A whitewater stream brought clean snowmelt down from the mountaintops to the dirty river we had just crossed. Rugged canyon walls rose on either side. Outcroppings of ancient rock stood, blistered by summer's heat and fissured by winter ice.

We shrugged into our packs and headed upstream into the canyon, away from the river. Watching the hillsides as we walked, we glimpsed a group of mule deer does and fawns. Browsing low on the hill, they had spotted us and were keeping their distance, using a row of scrubby trees for cover. They were on a faint outline of a trail that tore away from the creek bottom and we followed it up the north wall, finding the campsite.

It was low on the shoulder of the hillside, a semi-flat ridge leading to an outcropping of rock over-looking the stream. Across the canyon, on the north-facing slope, exposed to less direct sunlight, the succulent plants and grasses that bear search for in early spring were green and thick. Scanning the hillside with binoculars, we examined each blackened stump and moss-covered boulder, searching for a bear until we were satisfied that the bruins were holed up for the day.

We pitched the tent on a slight downhill angle, the closest we could come to flat ground. A light wind blew up the canyon and we unloaded our packs, grabbing a bite to eat in the morning sun. "Chuk-chuk-chuk." There were chukars calling. We looked around, trying to spot them. I picked one out, sitting on top of a boulder 75 yards (68 m) away and pointed him out to my buddy.

Dan caught a glimpse of movement from higher on the mountain and swung his binoculars to his eyes. There were six bighorn sheep staring down at us from 800 yards (728 m) away. All rams. They had been bedded when we arrived, watching us the whole time. Now some stood, some fed, turning their heads from time to time, watching us watching them.

They were lying in direct sunlight at the very top of a rock slide. A high, fissured cliff protected them from above and six pairs of eyes watched for danger's approach from the sides or below. There were two rams in the group whose immense horns and bodies dwarfed the rest of the herd. From carefully selected beds they could watch the other sheep and our camp for any signs of danger.

But we were there to hunt black bear and soon our attentions turned to the green slope opposite. We loaded our rifles and began the long climb around a cliff on our side of the canyon to achieve a better vantage from which to scan for bears. Each step was carefully taken. A loose stone might roll underfoot, a handhold could give way or a rattlesnake might be coiled beneath a ledge. We followed a sheep trail up, picking our way across rock slides, clutching at clumps of grass to keep balance on the treacherous slopes.

Up the canyon and high above camp now, we scanned the far hillside. More black rocks and lightning charred stumps and green grass and flowers. Not a bear to be seen. We turned our attention to our own slope once more.

Two more rams were feeding less than 200 yards (182 m) away. We were above them this time and they browsed along the hillside above a sheer drop of 200 feet (61 m). From this range we could see what they were feeding on, broad-leafed yellow flowers, bitterbrush and wild parsley. They were aware of us, stopping to watch for a moment, then dropping their heads to resume feeding. They moved toward us as they fed, then the biggest one, a full-curl ram in the prime of his life, scraped out a bed in the sun and laid down. The smaller half-curl ram continued to feed. Throughout the next three days we would never be very far from these bighorn rams, seemingly unconcerned with our activities yet always aware of our presence.

On Sunday we spotted a bear feeding on the far slope, high above us. The bear was black as night, by himself and feeding unconcernedly. We closed the distance, scrambling along a sheep trail carved out of a cliff. Hanging on by clumps of grass and bitterbrush, we detoured around a rattlesnake den to flop down on our bellies, guns at the ready. A missed shot sent the bear running uphill and out of sight.

Pack a lunch and commit to hunting all day long. The deeper into the backcountry, the better.

# BY BICYCLE FOR BLACK BEAR

Though road closures prohibit motor vehicle access in some areas, a bicycle can help the hunter access good hunting far beyond the gate.

When I was young and just learning the ways of game and forest, road closures were unheard of. We drove any road we wanted to, parked where we wished and hiked from there.

That was then and, frankly, we saw less game in those days. Forest road closures have changed that, and the face of hunting is changing. On the negative side, many hunters don't have access to all hunting areas. On the positive side, game is less harried. The more distance a hunter can put between himself and a traveled road, the more game he is likely to see.

Walking beyond a closed gate on public land allows the hunter to see more country and more game. If you can cover ground faster, you will see even more country, and potentially, even more game. One way to cover a lot of ground in a hurry is on a mountain bike. A bike is not standard hunting equipment for most hunters yet, but many people are finding out just how useful they can be for putting distance between themselves and other hunters.

Mine has a carbon fiber frame, wide pedals to hold the tread of my hunting boots, 27 hill-climbing speeds, knobby tires, fenders, and a rifle rack.

A mountain bike, properly equipped, can carry water and food, a weapon, tent and sleeping bag, even the bear (or parts of it). Bow and rifle racks are mounted to the handlebars and can be purchased at bike shops and sporting goods stores.

Next in order of importance is a way to carry extra gear. A rack mounted behind the seat is a handy place to carry game bags, rope, camera, and lunch. A water bottle mounted to the frame can be a lifesaver on a hot day. Another necessary piece of equipment is a lock and chain. This ensures the bike will still be there at the end of the hunt, and not be pedaled down the trail by some boot-weary hiker.

Be sure to have a battery-powered light mounted up front to light the way on moonless nights. A helmet is a good idea too. Because the weight distribution on the bike is changed with the extra gear, chances of a spill are increased.

— Gary Lewis

## Landowners

Some of the best bear habitat is the best human environment. Where the four cornerstones of habitat—food, water, shelter and escape cover—come together, both bears and humans find the best living. Many property owners are happy to share their land with the bears. They tolerate raiding of the gardens and destruction of apple trees and ornamental plants because they enjoy catching a glimpse of Mr. Bruin. Other landowners call the authorities the first time a garbage can is tipped over or a bear gets into the dog food.

Almost everyone who lives on the edge of civilization in bear country has a story to tell. And most of these people are bear lovers. But the bear/human relationship is tenuous and, from time to time, the bear is not a good neighbor.

For the careful, ethical hunter, there are an abundance of opportunities to hunt bear on private land. While deer and elk hunting bring in paying clients for many landowners, bears do not. In fact, the more bears that are removed from a property, the better both the deer and elk hunting will get.

Let it be known that you are interested in hunting bears and invitations will follow. Cultivate these relationships. If you're allowed to hunt, take the time to send out a thank-you note when you get home, whether or not you bag a bruin. Stay in regular contact after the hunt and before the next one. If a new bear shows up or a neighbor starts having a problem, you'll be the one they call.

## Timber Companies

Because bears do a lot of damage to younger trees, timber companies are often happy to let bear hunters have access to large blocks of forest land. Maps show what areas are owned by Forest Service or Bureau of Land Management and which properties are owned by private companies. After selecting a hunt area with a high concentration of bears, contact the timber companies in the area. The worldwide web is one source of information on land ownership. Signs posted at entrance gates may give telephone numbers for information. And the small general stores that serve logging communities also serve as clearinghouses of information. Proprietors know who owns what land and, in some instances, where a hunter is likely to find bears.

In most cases, a timber company representative is not likely to hand over the keys to the gates. Access will probably be limited to walk-in or bike-in traffic. If in doubt, ask what modes of transportation are permissible.

Road Closed. A familiar sight in much of the West. But limited access reduces competition from other hunters.

A large boar above an old gravel quarry. Here, the bear found shade in the tall timber and fed on tall grass along the abandoned roadways.

## Social Filters

There are many factors that discourage access to some of the best hunting habitat. We call them social filters. We're programmed by traffic lights, crosswalk signals, yellow lines and Do Not Enter signs to stay with the crowd, in tune with civilization. So road closure signs keep hunters out, when it is often acceptable to go in afoot or on a bicycle.

Most people also stop or turn around at a gate, even if it is a gate that is open for passage to the public. In western states, with a high percentage of public ground, there are often cross fences to keep cattle from mixing on range land. If it is all public land, you are free to hunt beyond the gate. Go in on foot or by vehicle, but leave the gate the way you found it.

Find gated roads on the topo map. These may be permanently closed to vehicles. Watch the roadbed, ditches, banks and intersecting trails for bear tracks and scat. Scarred trees, torn grass, shredded stumps and rotten logs all can be indicators of recent bear activity.

Also, fear of fire may keep gates closed to timber company lands in low-water years, with "No Access" signs posted until the rains come.

In the same way, No Trespassing signs discourage hunting, when, if asked, a landowner might be perfectly happy to allow a bear hunter on her land. It has worked for me.

Rimrock and elevation changes also curb a hunter's enthusiasm. It's easier to park on level ground and hunt not far from the road. Distance is another social filter. Most people aren't in very good shape. To the determined hunter, any obstacle that nature has placed in the way is a gift. A hunter who walks in a mile (1.6 km) or more will put a lot of distance between himself and the rest of the camouflaged crowd. Study a topo map to find the areas with the greatest distance between roads.

For the same reasons, a lack of parking places is another social filter. One of my favorite hunting places has few places to park. Adjacent to the best spot there are no parking places at all. If you want to hunt it, you have to walk a quarter mile down the road to get there. Most people won't do that, parking at one end of the road or the other.

Herds of cattle also limit hunter numbers. But for the bear hunter, a herd of cattle is like bait on the hoof as Oregonian Dan Turpin found out. It was opening day of deer season and he followed a trail up the canyon on an old logging road. Tall timber kept the trail in shadow and groundwater helped the ferns stay green, even in early October. Turpin found where a buck had rubbed his antlers on some willows and began to look for the tracks.

Pounding hooves caught his attention. Something was coming fast. He settled in behind a fallen tree for cover. A herd of cattle lumbered into view. A young calf galloped at the rear of the herd. Right on its heels was a bear.

"If I'd hesitated another moment I could have had a bear and T-bone steaks," he said later.

Turpin, armed with a bear tag and a Remington 30-06, had a moment's decision. Should he take the shot and risk alarming the buck he was hunting? Or let the bear pull the calf down? He took the shot when the wide-eyed, bawling beef and the bruin were less than 25 yards (23 km) away.

Forest fires also discourage most hunters. For years, they'll avoid hunting an old burn. They assume since there is a high preponderance of charred timber that there is no food there and no wildlife. They are wrong. In the first five years after a burn, the new growth is astounding. Elk, deer and bear move into the burn to take advantage of the forbs and grasses that take off without the sun-blocking over-story. In the years that follow, as the blackened timber falls to the ground, bears find grubs in the rotten logs and huckleberries get a good start in the tops of burned-out stumps.

Oddly enough, Bear Danger signs are also social filters. If people don't camp there because of the danger posed by Old Bruin, chances are that the hunting is good.

Rivers and lakes are also social filters that keep most hunters out of land that is open to hunting. Once, we hunted timber company land behind a locked gate. We had permission to be there, but no key for the lock. Instead of walking in for miles to get back to the area we wanted to hunt, we used a boat to cross a lake and end up at a creek-bottom drainage.

We'd walked in a hundred yards from the water, up a skidder trail and spotted a bear coming toward us through the alders and blackberries. I let him get within 25 yards (23 m) and dropped him with one round from my .338.

Waders, a raft, a canoe, a jet boat—whatever it takes to put that barrier between the hunter and his fellow man, use it. Remember, bears don't do well around people. Get beyond the social barriers erected by man and nature and you will find better hunting.

A medium-sized river on Prince of Wales Island in Alaska. In the fall, the spawning salmon draw black bear from the surrounding drainages.

My brother and I were watching a clearing at the end of a closed road, west of Eugene, Oregon. At the far end of the clearing, we could see a bright green patch of grass, about 2 acres (0.8 hectare) in size. It was all clover, very short, and the elk had found it. While we scanned the rest of the clearcut, we kept an eye on the elk. Suddenly, the elk began to move, and in less than a minute they were gone and a sow with a pair of yearling cubs took over the patch of clover.

We watched them for awhile and they moved off. It was evening now and we stopped watching that area because it was directly into the sun and we couldn't see with the glare in our glasses. We concentrated on other areas and finally found another bear by itself that looked pretty small. We were looking for a bigger bear, so we didn't make a stalk on this one.

The sun had gone down far enough now that it was behind the hill. I looked back at the clover patch and could see something black in the middle of it. This one looked short-legged and rounder than the others.

A westerly coastal breeze was blowing, so we ran down the edge of the clearing on the inside of the timber along a rutted elk trail and came down over the top toward the patch. The bear would be below us now, we guessed. But there were three

bears. The biggest of the bears had a nice pelt. I shot it. At the impact, the bear dropped then bounced back up and went down into the drainage into the creek bottom. It was pretty easy to follow the track because there was a lot of fresh foliage that had been disturbed and lots of blood on both sides of the trail. We found the bear in the creek.

That clover was one of the few food sources that early in the season and since we knew where to find it, we were in place when the bears chased the elk away. We went back a couple of weeks later with a friend of mine and he shot another bear in the same spot. This one was even bigger, an old bear with a scarred-up face and an abscess.

That fall, we hunted back in the same area. All the big rotted stumps had huckleberries growing in the tops. We went back to that same clear cut and saw more than twenty bears over the course of a long weekend.

This spot was hot, both spring and fall for all the right reasons: It was at the end of a closed road, gated with a 3-mile (4.8 m) walk into the clearcut and the elk were having calves in that clearing. The creek bottom below had lots of skunk cabbage. In the fall, it held huckleberries. And there was water.

— Lee Van Tassell

This kind of evidence in swampy areas (left) is common proof that bears like skunk cabbage. Throughout the year (right), water is a vital part of survival.

## EVALUATING BEAR COUNTRY

Once you've checked your maps, conferred with biologists and determined accessibility, it's time to get outside. Scout your potential hunting areas, evaluate the availability of resources for the bear, and how you will run your hunt.

### Water Source

In the spring, water is not a critical factor. Of course, bears need moisture, but they find it in their foods, they find it in the trail and in rivulets in the canyons. As spring rains give way, however, to summer heat and the tinder-dry days of early fall, reliable water sources become very important.

One evening we were hunting deer in the coastal mountains on a parcel of private land on the edge of a small timber company holding. On the way back to camp, as the light faded from the canyon, we startled a bear coming down to water. When it heard us, it leapt into the deep, hidden pool. Soaked, it clambered out of the creek and turned to wait for us, less than 20 yards (18 m) away. Unable to see it in the shadows, I threw a stick and almost struck it, causing it to retreat a few more yards and turn again, ready to fight. We left it alone and headed back to camp.

In the summer and fall, bear need water every day. As the water sources dry up, the options become fewer and the chances of surprising a bear at a water hole go way up. Look closely to find their tracks around a pool. The soil may not give up a bear track easily in dry weather, but just at the water's edge, you may find the telltale pads and claw marks a bear leaves as it bends down for a drink.

Just because a creek goes dry doesn't mean that a bear can't find water there. Water may still remain in deeper pools that are hidden in the tangle of vines and deadfall. The bears know it's there. At this time of year, these creek bottoms may make easier walking when the water is low and pooled up instead of flowing bank-full with run-off.

In hot weather, a bear must stay closer to its water source and now is a good time to focus on foods that are nearby. If there are apples on the trees, check for scat and try to confirm what has been on the menu of late.

If there is a river close by, bears may come to the river in the early morning or late evening. Intercept them along the trails they use to move from feeding and bedding areas. This is when the ability to sit still for a few hours at a downwind stand can really pay off as the bears move out of the cover.

Author Lee Van Tassell with a big sow that he tagged in the fall. Even when bears aren't feeding on skunk cabbage, they can still be found in the vicinity because of the shade and moisture.

## Shelter, Cover and Travel Routes

To a lazy bear, the things that matter most are food, water and shade for temperature regulation. Often, cover is not far from feed in bear country. To a bear feeding in an old clearcut, a pile of cut limbs and uprooted stumps is a great place to take a nap during the midday hours and is also a potential winter den site.

Down in the bottom of the canyon, the habitat is even better. Here's where to find the bear trails where an animal can move about all day, unseen by humans and safe from cougars, wolves and other bears, its natural predators. Most canyons have seasonal streams that run for part of the year. Here the bear finds water and moisture and a little food.

Bears are most comfortable in forest habitats and some of the best cover is found in the stands of old growth timber left near a two- to five-year-old clearcut. That cool damp ground underneath the trees where the skunk cabbage grows draws in bear to rest during the day. Tall timber provides an escape for cubs and sows. Fallen trees create shade along the ground and the crater left by the root wad is another potential windbreak. Hollow logs and tree trunks are used all year for either beds or dens.

Except for the dominant animal in a given area, most bears live in fear of other bears, particularly during the mating season. Battles between males

are common. The struggle may be to the death, and the victor eats his rival. Examine the face of any larger bear and you are likely to see the scars of past scrapes.

In 2001, we hunted Prince of Wales Island, Alaska, where a friend of mine killed a boar that measured 7 feet, 6 inches (2.3 m) from nose to tail. Its nose and head were covered with fresh and healed-over marks of tooth and claw.

The cubs are vulnerable, too. In the spring, when a boar finds a sow with cubs, he may kill and eat the cubs to bring the sow into heat and back into the bedroom.

Subordinate boars, and sows with cubs are better off unseen. This is why they stay on the move throughout their core areas and take to cover at the first hint of danger. In brushy canyon bottoms in bear country, it's possible to find multiple trails that bears have carved out that enable them to keep their distance from other bears.

In the swamps, the most consistently used trails are the tunnels. Identify these hollowed-out passageways through the brush, and you'll find the bears using them year after year. In the summertime, when much of the fresh greens have dried up, the bears tend to focus their feeding efforts. If a bear knows he wants to eat berries, he'll head for the berry patch and he'll take the easiest trail to get there. Find the path of least resistance and you'll find the trails.

Lee Van Tassell (left) bagged this black bear while hunting coastal bears in Alaska with buddy Brant Hillman.

In old logging areas, you can find overgrown skidder trails coming down the ridgelines used by the loggers to move the timber out to the landings and onto the trucks. It takes many years for these scars to heal and the bear use them to move back and forth from feeding to bedding areas. Where the tall green grass grows alongside closed logging roads, bears feed as they move from one place to another. The alders are the first to grow up in the old skidder roads and the bears break them down to feed on the new growth.

There isn't as much cover in an area of re-production, where small trees have been planted to replace the timber harvest, but bears do use these young stands of timber for cover, especially during the spring.

Look for sign on the edges where the bear trails enter. If the sign is fresh, there's a good chance the bear is nearby. Try to find his escape routes, in and out of cover.

## Escape Routes

Though a few will stand and fight, the first thing most bears want to do when frightened or wounded is get away. If the bear is in a clearcut, it wants to get into heavy cover and it doesn't matter whether the nearest brush is uphill or downhill, that's where the bear is going.

Headed for cover at top speed, the bear has better control running uphill than going down. They seem to go much faster when they're going uphill. But you don't want to be below him when he decides to go down the hill. Sometimes a bear loses its footing and rolls, particularly if it is wounded, but it can come out of that tumble in a flash and light out on all fours once again.

If the bear is used to feeding in a particular place, chances are good it will use the same exit each time it leaves. If you begin to learn a bear's pattern and its exit strategy, you can set a partner there to cover the back door if you blow a stalk.

Whether the bear is headed up and out of the drainage, side-hill into a stand of old-growth, or down into the heavy brush along the creek bottom, it's going to go fast. But as soon as it makes it into cover and puts a little distance and a few obstacles between itself and danger, it slows down. A bear is not a long-distance runner. As soon as the immediate danger is averted, it slows down and conserves its energy.

Look for bears to use canyons and creek bottoms when moving from daily feeding to bedding cover. Where old growth timber has fallen or where burned trees have hit the ground, the bear may find a bed or burrow into a rotten stump. In old slash piles, a bear may tunnel-in to sleep.

The brush along a creek allows a bear to move virtually unseen, from the bottom of the drainage to its top. The bear knows it is more vulnerable on the side hill where the brush isn't as thick. So it stays down in the thick brush as much as possible whether it is just moving through, or on the run.

Roll out the topo map and find the feeding areas, then mark out the contour lines that point to saddles and up into the finger draws. Bears are fundamentally lazy. These are the travel lanes and, when danger threatens, these are the escape routes that a bear uses to move at high speed to safety. They'll hit the panic button a lot sooner if the hunter tries to cut corners by hunting with the wind.

## Prevailing Wind

A bear lives by his nose. If the breeze brings him news of food, sometimes he'll trail it for miles (km). A boar seeks out a mate by testing the wind for the smell of a sow in heat. A sow scent-checks to round up her cubs when it's time to move. And if the bear senses danger on the wind, she doesn't wait around to get a second opinion. On scouting trips, check the prevailing wind that whistles down a canyon and mark it in a journal or on the map. This kind of information comes in handy when it comes time to plan the still-hunt, set a bait or run the strike dogs.

In mountain country, the temperatures are generally warmer in the valleys and cooler on the ridge tops. In the morning, as temperatures rise, convection currents carry the wind uphill. In late afternoon and evening, the breeze may blow downhill as the weather cools.

Bait hunters should pay close attention to the prevailing wind when choosing a bait site. A bear won't find the bait until he smells it first. This could take anywhere from 90 minutes to two weeks, depending on the number of bears in the area and the prevailing wind. The wind may come out of one direction during the night and from the opposite way during legal shooting hours. Identify the prevailing wind direction and locate

Dry-country bears come in all colors, from blonde to brown and basic black. Hunts may take place in the spring, late summer and fall. The highest success rate comes from forested areas at high elevations.

the bait station to take advantage of the wind that will bear the good news of the bait during daylight hours.

A still hunter can never hope to beat a bear's nose while hunting with the breeze. The odds go way up when the hunter puts his nose in the wind, negating the bear's ability to smell him.

The hunter with a call, likewise, must pay special attention to the way the wind is blowing and to the scent left at the call site. Where legal, use cover scent and set attractant scent downwind.

## ASSESSING BEAR SIGN

What can a hunter learn from tracks, droppings and other bear sign? What should a bear hunter know about tracking?

If there is snow on the ground and the sign is fresh, the hunter should be able to track the animal. Other sign, such as prints in the soft ground along the trail, hair stuck in the fence and scat left behind all give clues about a bear's core area. The patient and observant hunter can learn a lot about the animal and, eventually, put together enough of the puzzle to decide where to set an ambush.

### Tracks

In forests with thick cover, black bear travel established trails and old logging roads and leave their tracks for the hunter to find. The tracks can help a hunter determine where that bear was feeding and give an indication of where he might be found again.

A black bear is a wide-bodied animal that moves both legs on one side of the body at a time as it walks. Like a human walker, the heel of the back foot lands flat on each step. In fact, the bear's back foot track is not dissimilar to a human footprint, but a bear's foot is shorter and wider. There are five toes on both front and rear feet. A bear's outer toe is the biggest. Often, the front foot's heel pad won't register in a track.

Bears come in many sizes and a mature bear may continue to grow until it is seven to ten years old,

This bear was feeding on a series of food types. Note the rabbit fur in the freshest droppings.

The tender green shoots of grass, before and after.

so it is difficult to judge a bear based on its track, but you can learn from experience by measuring the paws of bears you take and the tracks of bears along the trail. I measured the paws of a bear I took in Alaska. This bear measured 5 feet, 6 inches (1.7 m) from nose to tail. A five-year-old sow, its track is representative of other bears its size. From tip of the longest claw to the heel pad, its front foot measured 8 inches (20.3 cm) long. Its rear foot measured 7³/₄ inches (19.7 cm).

The trail width between the outer edges of a black bear's footprints averages 14 inches (35.5 cm). Measured from the tip of the foremost toe on one foot to the tip of the same toe on the other side, the black bear's stride averages 18 inches (47.5 cm) at a walk and between 2 and 5 feet (0.6 and 1.5 m) on the run.

The bear can run up to 30 miles per hour (48 kmph) in short distances, but its running tracks won't last for more than a few hundred yards (m). Walking slowly again, the hind foot overlaps the front foot. When a bear is walking fast, the hind foot lands in front of the front foot.

The large claws leave marks wherever the pads and toes do. In the muskeg found in coastal Canada and along the Alaska beaches, the bears walk trails that are centuries old. Their claw marks can be found where they've dug into the skunk cabbage or climbed a slope. In mud on a steep

bank, the bear leaves slide marks and scrapes where it loses traction. The same thing happens on ice and snow.

## Scat

Black bear droppings contain hints at where to find the bear. If a bear is eating berries or other fruits, the droppings may be a shapeless splat or shaped a little like an apple fritter, though not quite as tasty. When firm, black bear scat is tubular, between 1³/₈ inches (3.5 cm) and 1¹/₂ inches (3.8 cm) in diameter. A grizzly bear's scat has a diameter of over 2 inches (5 cm).

Consistently large piles concentrated in one area mean that there is a very big bear. I have seen some smaller bears produce some large piles, but in general size holds to size. To hunt bear, hunt the food source. Consistently large diameter scat, in dry country, means a bigger bear. And there's no better way to tell what a bear is feeding on than to find its fresh scat.

The content of fresh droppings may reveal that a bear was eating grass, or finding grubs in rotten logs and stumps. The scat contains plant matter such as grass stalks, seeds, roots, berries, nuts, buds, bark and leaves. These items may be mixed in with other tasties such as insects, eggs, mice, birds, chipmunks, ground squirrels, fish or honeycomb.

In Alaska, we found the ground-up shells of steamer clams just above the water line. The bears had been dining on the bivalve mollusks and tiny crabs. Don't be surprised to find bits of just about anything in a pile of bear scat. These clues may lead you to a feeding area.

Bears with a small home territory use the same spots to leave the evidence. Find a bear's droppings in the spring along an old trail and you'll probably find his sign there again in the summer, with bits of elk hair. In the fall, you'll find it laden with blackberry seeds and still later, with digested plums and apples.

## Bear Trees

A black bear uses trees to take refuge and as signposts to advertise their presence and size to other bears. Watch for smooth, worn bark and claw marks on the trunk. The bear may also scratch himself there, wearing the bark smooth and leaving bits of hair behind.

I've found more bear claw marks on trees on travel routes where more than one bear would use the trail. I'll find claw marks on alders and aspens. Whether or not, the bear is using the tree as a sign post to warn other bears, it serves as a good indicator of the size of the bear in the area.

Sometimes a bear knocks down a small tree. Whether it is to warn another bear or announce its presence or because it is in the way, it's hard

Territorial markings on a tree in Idaho show the bear's size and confirm that this is a boar's home territory.

to know. Whenever I've seen a bear slap down a small tree, it has always been a big old boar.

On the Pacific coast, by the fourth week of spring, the sap is running in the hemlock trees. By this time, the bear's appetite is whetted for something to supplement his diet of grass. With his claws, he hooks into a tree and tears off a slab of bark, laying bare the trunk. Pressing his wide-open mouth against the tree, he scrapes his upper and lower front teeth up and down into the sap-soaked cambium layer (new growth ring). A sticky, spongy mass accumulates behind his teeth and he stops to scrape it off with his tongue and swallow. The process continues, the bear ripping off more bark and scraping the cambium until he is satisfied. If he completes a circuit around the tree, completely girdling it, the tree will die.

If a bear really likes what he's getting from a particular tree, he may skin it all the way to the top, leaving a shining, barkless, tooth-scarred snag as evidence. Bears will, in general, peel trees from 3 inches (7.6 cm) to 3 feet (0.91 m) in diameter. Larger trees are peeled in the tops where the bark is thinner. Binging bears have been known to peel up to forty trees a day.

Later in the spring, the sap is running in cedar, fir trees, white pine, alder and spruce. For a change of taste, the bears move out of the hemlocks and attack new stands of trees.

## Grubbing

Keener than almost any animal, a bear's sense of smell is what he uses to find his groceries. It's hard to find a food that a bear will not eat. Fresh meat is at the top of the list, but insects and larvae are not far behind.

Once I watched a bear walk a beach in the evening. He emerged from the tree line at low tide and stayed at least ten yards from the water. He grazed on the tender grasses, then stood on his back legs to reach the new shoots on the willows, then tipped over rocks to eat whatever grubs he could find. Every few yards (meters) he found something new to eat.

Bear, scratching his back on a tree. Hair can be found where the bear rubbed and height can indicate size as well.

In tidal pools, bears can find small crabs, clams, mussels, sand worms, kelp and a host of other chow brought in with the tide. The evidence is in the scat found just inside the tree line. Every beach, everywhere we hunted on Prince of Wales Island had a trail just inside the tree line, well tracked by deer, bear and wolves.

A hunter can locate evidence of grubbing wherever black bears live. The larvae of a multitude of different creatures are up for grabs. Look for old stumps with blueberry or huckleberry bushes growing out of the tops. Bears are looking for these as targets of opportunity to dig out ants, grubs or bees. Bee hives are especially tasty and the scent of the honey draws him in to the nests in hollow trees. A bear gobbles what he can get while he can get it. Termite nests too, after the insects have riddled a rotten log with their excavations, are another mark for a roving bear.

In dry climates, it is common to see a bear in a grassy meadow turn from eating grass to flipping over rocks. All kinds of creatures hide under boulders and they're all on the menu.

On the hunt, or a scouting trip, watch for stones that have been tipped over. On forestlands where ranchers run cattle, keep a lookout for dried cow flops that have been flipped on their tops. Chances are good the bear found what he was looking for.

## Hair

Bears rub on boulders and fence posts. In such places, you'll find long black or brown or blonde cylindrical filaments left in the cracks. Where bears have climbed trees or scratched their backs on hemlock trees, the long black hairs will be left in the bark. Hunting in Washington, we found bear hair stuck in the thorns of the devil's claw. In Alaska, we found the bear hair on the branches of the willows on well-used trails.

Where two bears have fought, they'll leave the evidence behind in hair scattered around the scene of the battle. And at the entrance to a suspected den or a bear tunnel, the telltale hairs will be caught on thorns or pinched in the bark.

Barbed wire is another good place to find bear sign. Bears have little regard for a barbed wire fence. They'll go under it, over it or through it, whichever is easiest. And they go fast, especially when there's food on the other side. Bear trails in cattle country are punctuated by barbed wire. Their crossings are marked by long black hairs. Where a bear goes through a fence, he'll leave a little bit of hair behind.

Black bear don't come easy, but tracks, scat, trails and feeding signs found while scouting can tell a story. Find these clues in bear country and the insights and patterns begin to emerge that will help put a bear in the sights. The next step is strategy.

# CHAPTER THREE

# Hunting Strategies

**T**ake a look at typical bear habitat. Here is dense undergrowth, dark timber and grassy meadows laced by streams and swamp. On the slopes above, there are timber sales and new growth and blown-down, rotting trees. Where does the hunter start?

## SPOT AND STALK

Bears spend the first weeks out of hibernation eating grass, skunk cabbage, wildflowers and the buds on tree branches in order to get their stomachs working again after the long sleep. In the fall, the berries ripen on the mountain tops and in old burns and clearcuts. Elk prefer calving in sunny clearings. Much of what a bear wants to eat can be found in the open and this is what makes spot and stalk a viable strategy.

Bears don't keep regular schedules. Old Bruin might feed out in the open at first light and then lay down in the tall grass for the rest of the morning. As the sun warms the grass, he might roll over, stretch his legs or find a shady spot beneath a tree. If the bear sign says there have been bears in the area within the last week then sitting still to watch a far hillside will do more for putting sausage on the table than walking every road.

Sitting still takes a mindset change. Our natural inclination is to stay on the move, but a bear's sense of smell and its hearing are so attuned to its environment that a hunter's movement in a bear's habitat compromises the chance of a sighting. Set up ideally with the sun at your back and the wind in your face. If the wind is wrong, find someplace else to hunt.

# BUMBLEBEE BLACK

The spring bear hunt (top) is a lazy time when the sun warms the hillsides, where a few weeks ago, snow blanketed the mountain. Now there are wildflowers and the green grass bends with the gentle breeze.

It was one of those days, later in the season, when I'd hunt alone. None of my regular partners could get time off work to go with me. I left well before first light and parked at a gated road and hiked far into the timber to a place I'd scouted early in the season. It was a series of small clearcuts that were about three to five years old. There was some grass growing in patches on the hillsides and the bears had been feeding there since early April. I set up the spotting scope and began to scan the slopes across the canyon.

About 1½ miles (2.4 km) away, three bears worked in a clearing. Any one of them was big enough to shoot, but getting in range took me most of the day. By the time I got there, the bears had vanished. I guessed that by evening, they'd be back out feeding again.

A closed logging road went through the creek bottom. I crossed the creek and walked a little way to sit on a high point, only 75 yards (68 m) from a little swamp full of skunk cabbage and tall grass. Several bear tunnels led out onto the logging road. Sitting down, I rested the .45-70 across my lap. With any luck, a bear would show before night fell.

After a few minutes, I began to hear limbs popping and cracking and lots of bear sounds—moans, wheezes and grunts. The leaves of a fern were moving every so often. I couldn't figure out why an animal would stay in one spot and just move this one fern. When I tracked him later, it turned out that he was digging out a bumblebee nest on a root wad in an old shaky stump and eating the grubs in the nest.

The bear finished up with the nest and I could see a patch of black moving through the skunk cabbage. But when it came out into the road it caught my scent on the ground. He stopped stock-still like something had slapped him in the face. I knew the gig was up.

I was about 70 yards (63.7 m) away and I swung up the rifle and shot the bear right in the sternum with a 300-grain Nosler Partition. After the sound of the shot died away, all was quiet. Then a second bear bolted away. I didn't know there was more than one bear. I waited twenty minutes to see if I could hear anything then walked down to where I'd shot and there was the bear, stone cold dead.

Getting there I'd made quite a bit of noise breaking through the brush. When I found the bear, I began to clear out some limbs to get ready to gut and skin the animal. I heard a sound less than a hundred yards away and looked up to see the second bear looking right at me. It only moved away after I yelled at it.

I would never have seen those bear without taking the time to use the spotting scope. At the kinds of distances we hunt in the western canyons, binoculars don't have the reach to probe into the shadows and gullies. Also, using a spotting scope encourages the hunter to scout in advance, and to pick the best habitat and vantage point.

When it comes to gear, buying good glass is the single best investment that the spot and stalk hunter can make.

Lance Manske with his eye to the spotting scope. In open country, good, full-size optics and the patience to use them are a must.

## Use of Optics

Optics help you find the right black bear. And most often you don't take the first bear you find. You need a closer look, and because bears are so wary, good optics are a must. If a trophy is desired, the game becomes even more difficult. Optics and patience are the keys to success.

Binoculars first. Pick a pair that represents the best choice you can afford (see Optics, Chapter 4). For the hunting binocular, a seven-power is a good minimum choice with an objective lens of 35 mm to 50 mm. On the high end of magnification, choose a ten-power with an objective of 50 mm.

Mounted on a tripod, the scope or big binoculars are mandatory in big country. Among a group of three hunters, there should be at least one spotting scope. At 800 yards (728 m), dialed up to 45x, a black boulder might turn out to be a sleeping bear.

The best use of optics is to start by scanning the target area with the binoculars, closest area first, working to farther away. Look at every boulder or stump and fix its location in mind relative to landmarks. After the first thorough search with the binoculars, switch to a spotting scope or astronomical binoculars.

With the spotting scope set at 15x-20x, search the hillside using an imaginary grid pattern. Start at one side and pan slowly across, make a slight adjustment up and pan back. With each movement of the scope, start at the top of the field of view and scan in a circle. Finish the grid and start over again. To examine something in more detail, dial the scope up to maximum.

Neil Lewis, glasses openings in the timber on an evening hunt. The success of spot-and-stalk tactics depend on patience.

Take a break from the scope from time to time to allow the eyes to rest before a headache starts. If there are more hunters than spotting scopes, rotate the privilege. If the area under surveillance is more than 300 yards (273 m) away, it's okay to move around a little, perhaps to check for activity in a nearby canyon. But practice stillness. On a bear hunt, patience pays off more often than not.

Once a bear is spotted, take time to watch and formulate a plan. How big is the bear? Is it a sow with cubs? Is the hide rubbed? Are there other bears or other animals such as deer and elk between the hunter and the target? Find a route that makes the best use of the terrain and the wind and scan every bit of it with binoculars. Spook something else on the way in and you run the risk of blowing the bear out of the canyon before you are close enough for a shot.

## Judging Distance

Clear air, canyons, tall grass and timber make judging distance difficult in the mountains. Add the environmental factors to the inherent difficulties of judging bears and the result is a lot of arrows that shoot low or high and

rifle bullets that plow into the dirt beneath a bear's belly.

Very few people are good at judging distances beyond 50 yards (45.5 m). Ask any group of hunters how far away that pine tree is and you'll get as many different answers as there are tongues to wag. And almost all of them are wrong. In fact, the best I've seen at judging distance was a friend of mine who spends hundreds of dollars every month in greens fees and tournament entries. All those days on the golf course looking at the flags on whippy poles and driving a little white ball have made him a very good judge of distance.

The best practice off the golf course is with a rangefinder. At the range and out in the field, make the use of lunch breaks and down time to estimate distances to different targets. Pace them off or use a rangefinder to verify.

A common way to compensate for lack of skill in judging distance is to use a flat-shooting rifle, but at distances beyond 300 yards (273 m), a miscalculation of just 50 yards (45.5 m) can make the difference between a hit and a miss even with a high velocity load and a lighter bullet. Closer is always better.

Jennifer Lewis on a fall bear hunt in dry, open country (above). Author Lee Van Tassell, with his .45-70, on a driftwood-covered beach, glassing for bear (right).

## Terrain Assessment and Sketching the Stalk

One of the realities of bear habitat is that it never looks the same up close as it does from across the canyon. Downed trees, boulders, piles of slash, berry bushes and patches of ferns are not only landmarks, but obstacles. When the brush is higher than your head, the stalk can stall without further input from a spotter across the way.

Before the stalk begins, assess the terrain for foliage type, obstacles, and bare ground. Then look closer to detect the gullies, creeks, washes and the less obvious folds in the ground that allows for an undetected approach.

On a note pad, sketch the terrain features, the position of the animal and the possible approaches. With a sketch in hand, the hunter no longer has to rely on  memory, but can refer to the plan when suddenly everything begins to look different from the way it looked through the spotting scope.

Divide the route into separate short legs based on types of concealment which necessitate a single type of movement technique. Depending on the situation, the stalk may have one leg or half a dozen, depending on the cover and the distance. Use a range finder to estimate distance from observation point to landmarks along the route.

On the stalk, it isn't necessary for the stalker to see the target. In fact, it is counterproductive to stop for a look at the bear. Instead, the hunter should let a spotter keep watch. On the stalk, the hunter can turn to look at the spotter for confirmation of the route and status of the target.

## Signal System

There's no reason to hurry the stalk if the bear isn't on the move. If the animal beds down in view, the stalk could take the better part of a day. On the other hand, some bears feed at a fast pace and cover a lot of ground while they're putting on the feed bag. In these cases, plan the stalk to put the hunter where the bear is going, to intersect the trail at a saddle or the top of a canyon where the terrain funnels game into a narrow area.

If the distance is 800 yards (728 m) or less, leave one hunter at the spotting scope to direct the action. If the bear moves, the spotter can relay the information by hand signals.

This system of hand signals was developed by noted outdoor writer Ed Park to use for communicating visually across hundreds of yards. Working out the details before you begin your stalk will pay dividends when the animals (seemingly) disappear. Both hunters should have binoculars. Carry these instructions and pass them out to hunting partners so that everyone speaks the same sign language.

- Holding rifle or bow overhead means I want signals or I'm sending signals.

- Number of fingers indicates size of animal.

    A. Moose—Palm and fingers extended.

    B. Sheep—Crazy signal (finger rotating around ear).

    C. Bear—Bite hand.

    D. Deer—Two fingers above head (doe— wave palm over head).

- Distance—hold hands apart as appropriate; 1 foot = 100 yards (30 cm = 91 m).

- Hat on head means nothing has changed. The animal or animals are still in position and haven't moved far from the time when they were spotted and the stalk began.

- Direction—To indicate direction of travel or the direction of a target or non-target animal, stand and hold arms to show the direction as if on a clock face. For example, if the bear is up the hill and slightly to the right of the stalker, the spotter will hold his arms in the 1 o'clock position.

- Target gets away—wave arms.

## The Stalk

In the modern world, far from the realities of hunting predators with sharp teeth and claws, we're barraged by media that promises instant gratification. We're conditioned to make impulse decisions and move fast, get the job done now and take on the next task. Consider by contrast the pace and the focus required for a bear hunt. There is only room for one idea, one focus. And the bear sets the pace. A bear hunter must develop a philosophy of stealth.

Stealth means slowing down, immersing yourself in small, deliberate actions that keep mind and body occupied and focused. To this end, each aspect of the stalk should be planned. The first aspect is movement. A stalk isn't about getting there fast, it's about slipping into position with the intention of never being seen, heard or smelled by the target bear or any other animals in the area.

On the stalk, walk erectly through tall woods or other screening cover when there is concealment from all but close range detection. Use a crouching walk when foliage is irregular and less than head high.

A high crawl is used when vegetation is low, the target is still far off and a hunter can keep his head above the grass. The elbow crawl is useful when the foliage is shorter. This move takes more time to cover ground.

With the low crawl, the hunter's belly is on the ground. At this point, movement is very slow and difficult. The rifle or bow must be strapped across the back or cradled on the arm.

The leopard crawl is slowest of all and is used when concealment is sparse, such as along a gravel bar or a beach. The hunter creeps on his belly, arms and legs outstretched, using fingers and toes to propel himself along, inches at a time. Fortunately, most stalks in bear habitats don't call for this extreme.

Don Lewis (top) with a big Alaskan boar that was aged at seven years. This bear fell to a .300 Winchester Magnum on a spot-and-stalk hunt.

Chad Schearer (bottom) took this Alaska bruin with a muzzleloader after a late-evening stalk on a windy beach.

# GETTING WITHIN RANGE

Once the bear is located, there are two options—and time is of the utmost importance. If the morning is late or the sun is on the horizon, the hunter must move fast. If the bear is nearby, the first option is to slip in close and make the shot. The other move is to plan an ambush. Unless the bear is disturbed by another hunter or another bear, it will probably return to feed in the same spot, using the same route traveled earlier in the day.

## Within Bow and Handgun Range

When the weapon dictates you hunt at close quarters, you want to scout out places where you know there are a lot of bears and the habitat allows for stalking and listening in a high-density area. Closed, greened-over logging roads in late summer are ideal when it is cool in the shade.

These lazy days are when you'll find bears that walk the road and eat the berries that are growing in the little bits of sunlight, or cross the trail going from bedding to feeding areas.

When the wind is right and the bear is occupied with feeding, a hunter can get within rifle range with little difficulty. When armed with a muzzle-loader, a handgun or a bow, the rules change. A 50-yard (15 m) shot is the ideal for the limited-range firearms and for an effective arrow kill, the distance should be less than 40 yards (36 m).

Every bear and every situation is different. To get within bow or handgun range, hunt where bear numbers are high and evaluate each opportunity. Some bears feed at a rambling walk, while others may stay in one place for several hours, allowing for a measured, considered approach.

A dominant boar had this tidal flat all to himself. The wind was always wrong for this hunt and the bear is still there (above).

Brian Thompson shows off his first black bear. This bear was spotted from over 1½ miles (2.4 km) away from the opposite hillside and stalked to within 50 yards (45.5 m) while it was feeding on new growth just below the snowline (opposite top).

From left to right: Lee Van Tassell, Rick Jamison, Brian Clark with a big boar. Rick used a .277 Jamison and a 130-grain Swift Scirocco (opposite bottom).

On a spot and stalk day, I prefer the morning watch over the evening, because once a bear is spotted, it may be kept in view for several hours while we wait for the wind to change or the animal to move into an area more suitable for a stalk.

Here's the time to evaluate the bear and its surroundings. What other animals are nearby? Bump a doe on the way in and she might blow or snort and alert the bear to trouble. Run into a sow with cubs on the way to a big boar and you might get more than you bargained for.

Take the time to scope out the trail and choose landmarks that you can use to close the gap while staying out of sight. Within 500 yards (455 m), use a rangefinder to locate different objects between you and the animal. If you know that that boulder is 475 yards (432 m) away and the bear beyond it is at 510 yards (464 m), then it should be an easy 35-yard (32 m) shot from the boulder.

When a stalk stalls because the hunter has run out of cover, a call can attract the bear's attention and bring the animal within range.

# THE HANDGUN HUNT

wanted to try out a new handload for my 44 Magnum Smith and Wesson 629. I'd worked up a load for a 300-grain hard-cast bullet with a wide meplat and a gas check and it seemed to perform well on paper from the 6-inch (15 cm) barrel.

It was late August and very hot and dry for the coast range. I decided to concentrate on a creek drainage that fed into a coastal lake. The area had been logged on the uphill side of a road that ran along the creek drainage. The main road was up high, but there was an old skidder trail that followed the creek and it was blocked at the access point. The only way in was on foot.

The road was very dusty and there were tracks everywhere. Deer, elk, ruffed grouse and turkeys were using the road to be close to water. I saw a lot of bear tracks but most of them were smaller, in the 150- to 200-pound (67.5 to 90 kg) range. The sunny side of the canyon was choked with salal and intermittent patches of blackberries and was inaccessible by vehicle.

After I'd hunted along the skidder road for a couple of hours, I heard some bear activity in the swamp below me. It sounded to me that the animal was working its way upstream away from the lake which would have taken it up to the clearcut where there were a lot of blackberries.

I was trying out some hearing enhancements and was trying to sort out all the different forest noises, but I could hear the bear. And it couldn't have been more than 75 yards (68 m) away. It was working through and feeding upstream. I tried to pinpoint its location and direction of travel and get in front of it.

There. Two tunnels emerged from the brush and trails crossed the dirt road. I picked out one of the tunnels and sat across from the opening, pulling my facemask down to keep the mosquitoes at bay.

The shadows began to lengthen and soon a half-hour had elapsed and I'd begun to lose interest. The bear had quit making noise. I began to question what I'd heard and second-guess my decision to sit here, but I knew better than to get up. Staying put has put more bears in front of me than moving.

Suddenly there he was. He'd come in quiet and had popped up about 10 yards (9 m) away and stood there, on all fours, looking right at me. His head was wide. A better handgun shot opportunity I couldn't have asked for. I eared back the hammer.

Hold 3 inches (7.6 cm) under the chin, I told myself. The fluorescent green fiber optic front sight really showed up against that black hair. About 2 pounds (0.9 kg) of pressure on the trigger.

At the shot, the bear reared and turned and went back where it had come from.

I heard a soft moan and waited 20 minutes more, then I crawled in to find it. The bank was very steep. I was crawling in headfirst with my gun in front of me and a Mini-Mag light. Suddenly, the ground gave way and I free-fell about 5 feet (1.5 m) and landed on top of the bear. It was stone dead, but it let out a "woof" when I hit it. That new bullet had done its job.

# CALLING BEARS

If there's one thing a hungry bear wants more than anything else, it's an easy meal. And he's used to taking food away from smaller predators.

When a prey animal is in distress, it cries out in distinctive, imitable ways. Bear calls are available that mimic these distress calls. Deer, elk, rabbits, squirrels and other rodents are all on a black bear's menu plan. If a prey animal is in trouble, it could very well signal that supper's on. There's nothing a bear likes better than an easy meal.

Jared Thomas (below right) and Wayne Endicott, bask in the glow of a hunt gone right. Taking a bear with a bow is a short-range encounter that, for a rush of adrenaline, is second to none.

This bear (below) was spotted from a boat. A skiff enabled the hunter, Lee Van Tassell, to put ashore downwind. Lee used driftwood and boulders to get within 80 yards (73 m) for the shot with his .300 Winchester Short Magnum and a 180-grain Nosler AccuBond.

# JENNIFER'S FIRST BEAR

Twelve-year-old Jennifer Lewis with the bear she took on the second day of her first big game hunt. Spot-and-stalk tactics gave way to a calling sequence that brought this bear in.

Above the river, the land rose gently. The slopes were carpeted with yellow grass and the feeder canyons were green with thorn and tangled vines. Above the valley floor, the ground sloped steep to the rimrock. Well-worn game trails intersected with paths once walked by Nez Perce ponies. On the skylines, red-barked pines stood tall against a cloud-scaled sky.

My daughter Jennifer, twelve years old at the time, wore a borrowed camo jacket with the hood pulled over the top of her red baseball cap. Over her coat she wore a blaze orange vest. She thumbed four rounds into her Ruger bolt-action and locked the bolt home on the empty chamber.

This morning we would hunt the river trail through the apple orchard, while Brent and Bitsy would walk parallel along the water. Tod would take the high ground, west of the river, where he could have a good view of the country ahead on both sides of the stream.

We'd walked 1/2 mile (0.8 km) when we found the first fresh sign. "Is that a bear track?" Jennifer whispered.

There, in the powdery dust was a track made some time this morning, its edges crisp and well-defined. Back-tracking the bear as we walked, I showed her the prints of the front and back feet and the places where the points of the claws dug into the dirt.

This second day of the hunt, it looked like we had made the right decision to work the river bottom. Grasshoppers had wiped out the hawthorn bushes on the slopes above. Whole groves of trees were stripped of leaves. The barren trees looked like winter, except for the hoppers clinging to the branches.

Now nature had gathered her creatures to the river bottom, where the apple and plum trees shed their fruit and the bushes still bore berries. We watched a doe and a fawn on the slope, then eased along the trail. In less than 1 mile (1.6 km), we found four different sets of bear tracks in the path and the tracks of deer.

I'd borrowed a FoxPro caller that I carried in my backpack. Maybe today, with so many deer in the canyon, it would pay off if a hungry bear thought he could steal an easy meal. My calls would imitate the sound of a deer fawn in distress. Music to a black bear's tastebuds. Black bear eat a lot of deer and elk in northeast Oregon.

After we'd walked more than a mile, we stopped to rest at the mouth of a draw. Downstream, I could see Brent and Bitsy. Across the canyon, Tod was visible beneath his orange hat.

Below us, the river made an easy turn. Hawthorn and apple trees grew on the opposite bank, shading a big gravel bar. And there, on the bar, was a bear. A chocolate brown black bear that walked downstream toward us with a swagger, his belly low to the ground.

"There," I whispered. "Across the river."

Jennifer bolted a round into the chamber and brought her gun up, but the bear kept moving and disappeared into the brush then emerged. In a moment he had vanished into the brush again.

Shrugging out of my pack, I grabbed the call. At the first fawn distress wails, the bear was out of the trees and back on the beach. With his head up, he plunged into the river, headed straight for us. I set the caller down and we backed up 20 yards (18.2 m). In less than a minute the bear crossed the trail and caught our scent. I saw the flash of fur as it passed the spot where we'd stood only moments before.

Now he climbed the hill, moving away. Jennifer dropped to her knee and shouldered her rifle. In a few moments he would hit the hawthorns and disappear. The bear paused on a rock outcropping and turned broadside. Jennifer, with her elbow on her knee and the gun against her shoulder, tightened her finger on the trigger. Thirty minutes later we stood over my daughter's first bear, a chocolate brown boar with a long-haired coat and laden with summer fat.

Back at the ranch house we skinned the animal and hung it in the shade. The girls picked apples while we rendered the fat into grease.

That evening we called in another bear that came looking for a deer fawn to eat. Across the river from where Jennifer took her bear, Tod bagged his, a black-haired boar with a diamond blaze.

It was a long, hard pack down the canyon through the stinging nettles and the thorns, but there were plenty of hands to help. And at 10:00 pm, after the day's second bear hung in the barn, we sat at the table and ate hot apple pie made with some of the freshest bear grease that ever graced a pie plate.

## The Setup and Call Sequence

Set up to call with both hunters watching in separate directions to cover each other's back. The call should be made from a vantage point that commands a good view, but is not too obvious. Bears are generally more willing to come downhill to a call, but they will climb a bank if they're motivated. Above all, keep the wind in your face.

When you have run out of cover on a stalk, a mouth call is the easiest to use. Don't go high volume with it though. A blast of sound is liable to send the bear out of the county. Instead, start softly and make the sound mournful and plaintive with a continuous wail. The drawback to a mouth call in this situation is that the bear pinpoints your position and comes in head-on, looking for food and a fight. Be ready to give it to him.

An electronic call, if it can be put into play with a minimum of trouble, can be positioned away from the hunter to allow for a crossing or broadside shot.

The predator call heightens the bear's awareness and raises the stakes. Everything changes when the call is used. The bear may turn aggressive, go passive, be curious or turn tail, depending on his hunger and place in the local hierarchy. But calling works often enough that it is a viable option that can bring a bear into bow or handgun range.

But bears have a short attention span. Mr. Bear is easily distracted. On the way toward a call, he may stumble across a berry patch or a spawning salmon. You need to keep the sound rolling to keep him on the move. Keep the calls constant—try to be subtle and he may lose interest.

Also, think bigger meals. There's a lot more protein in a deer than in a rodent or a rabbit. A fawn bawl gives a bear the prospect of seizing a bigger meal than it may get coming to the sound of a cottontail.

Lastly, give him time. Depending on how far he's got to travel, you may see the bruin in a few minutes or an hour. Do your scouting first to make sure there are bears in the area. Then keep the wind in your favor and your confidence high. Commit to spending an hour at each call set.

Remember that bears have a short attention span. Keep the call's wailing almost constant. When the sound trails off, a bear that might have been coming to the call, forgets about what he's heard and starts following his nose to the next meal. His nose, after all, is more reliable than his ears.

The ears are pointing in two different directions—one front and one back. The nose is up. Both are indications that this brown-phase bear has located the source of a sound to investigate.

The FoxPro electronic call was set on fawn distress. This call brought in two bears in one day. The first responded in less than a minute. The second emerged from the brush in 15 minutes.

The bear was on this gravel bar across the river when the hunters spotted it. It had vanished into the trees. When Lewis began to call, the bear emerged from the bushes and plunged straight into the river.

## Response to the Call

Every bear is an individual and may react differently from any other bear. At the sound of an animal in distress, a bear may turn an indifferent ear. Smaller bears are more likely to run away at the sound of the call because they don't have the life experience that tells them that something good to eat is squalling. Smaller bears also tend to be frightened by high-volume calls. Bigger bears show curiosity or outright aggressiveness.

We've seen dominant boars move quite aggressively to the sound of the call. We've also watched a dominant boar stop, sit down and simply listen to the sound for twenty or even more minutes.

Bears also show annoyance at the persistence of the call, eventually moving away from the sound. In open country, this type of behavior can pay off in a shot opportunity.

## Closing the Deal

An approaching bear expects to find something good to eat at the end of the trail. And he expects to have to fight for the meal. Fawn deer, for instance, only bawl when something is trying to eat them.

Don't expect the shot to be easy. The bear may charge across a meadow or it may come up through the brush. In either case, it is probably going to be on the move and may be coming head-on.

With a bear that is quartering head-on, hold one-third to halfway up the body between the head and the shoulder to punch the projectile through the scapula and the heart and lungs.

Sometimes a frontal head shot is all you get. From the front, break the bridge between the eyebrows. The neck is a hard one to shoot, because it is hard to break the spine without a perfectly placed shot, though, if the bear's head is up, it will put the bear down fast.

Here, author Gary Lewis uses the root wad of a downed tree as cover for a calling sequence.

Jennifer Lewis reenacts the shot while the author watches to see if the bear will reemerge from the hawthorn bushes.

When a bear such as this comes in to a call, a hunter better be ready to close the deal. By the look of this bear, he's a scrapper and he'll be ready for a fight.

When calling bears, a hunter is well-advised to have a partner to watch the opposite direction. Bears may approach on the run and with very little sound.

Going slow in a bay filled with icebergs. Even in June, when the days are long, the snowline is not far above the bay in Prince William Sound.

## BOAT-BASED BEAR HUNTS

In British Columbia and Alaska, boat-based bear hunts are a great option. Deep valleys, rugged coastline, firs and cedars, lakes, rivers and muskeg dominate this landscape. Because rainfall here is measured in feet (meters) rather than inches (centimeters), there is water everywhere. It is perfect habitat for bears and perfect for a hunter with a skiff.

Boat-based bear hunts operate out of several ports, including Seward, Whittier and Homer on the Kenai Peninsula, and out of Valdez, and Sitka. Hunts take place in and around the Chugach National Forest in Prince William Sound; and in southeast Alaska on Prince of Wales Island and surrounding islands. Boat hunts also operate out of ports in British Columbia.

The great thing about hunting from a boat is that the hunter is not locked in to one area. If there are few bears and too many hunters, just weigh anchor and move. The inlets and bays are beyond number and no human could climb all the hills

in a thousand lifetimes. From the water, the hunter can scan the bays and the shorelines and use optics to probe the open muskeg bogs and avalanche slides to locate the right bear.

The best spots to find bears are back in the bays. Watch for the mouths of the creeks. Here, the tide pushes back up the inlets and carries in the seafood. The black bears hunt out of the valleys and come out onto the beach at low tide to eat kelp and whatever else washed in with the surf. Early in the season, when the bears are fresh from their dens, they'll spend hours on the beach and can be seen at anytime of day. Later, as the days get warmer, bears come only to the water's edge in the evening and the morning, seeking shade when the sun is high.

One of the most important items to have in the boat is a book of tide tables. The bears come to the beach at low tide to feed on the food left by the sea and exposed among the rocks. When low tide coincides with evening or morning, on a day when the rain isn't pounding down, the hunting can be spectacular.

The tide is the hunter's friend and foe. A low tide can leave the party stranded for the day with the skiff a half-mile (0.8 km) from the water. A high tide can isolate a hunter on an island or outcropping of rock. Pick the wrong place to take a nap and you may find yourself swimming for shore. Pay attention to the high tide line when setting up to watch a lonely beach. And never turn your back on the sea.

Some people have the impression that hunters shoot from the skiff. It is against the law to shoot from a boat. The hunter must climb out of the boat, then load the gun and make the stalk.

A fringe benefit of the boat-based hunt is the fishing. Halibut, rock fish, shrimp and crab are all part of the potential catch and the menu, so don't forget to pick up the appropriate fishing licenses.

Adam Westfall, back at base camp with his black bear. Westfall spotted the bear from the boat and stalked it on shore.

## Guided or Transported?

In general, there are two types of boat-based black bear hunts available: guided or transported.

On a guided hunt, a hunter contracts with an outfitter who coordinates all the aspects of the expedition, including travel, meals, and licensing. The hunt itself may take place from the boat with the guide and clients scanning the beach with binoculars while cruising at a measured pace, or, the hunters go ashore to search some secluded valley. Usually it is some combination of the two methods. The guide makes the judgment call as to the best places to hunt and uses different methods to put the client in front of a bear. Depending on the location, baits or calls may be employed. When a bear is killed, the client may

be asked to assist in the skinning and the packing but all these tasks are generally the responsibility of the guide.

On a transported hunt, the hunter arranges with a transport company to get there and back. Meals are often the responsibility of the transporter. In the hunt area, it is the responsibility of the hunter to make the decisions where to hunt. Alaska state law makes it illegal for the transport employee to advise hunters in any aspect of the hunt that does not deal directly with transportation.

The transporter carries the hunter from the boat on a skiff to shore. His responsibilities and his obligations end at the beach. If a hunter engages a transport company employee in any aspect of the stalk, the employee's job is at risk and his employer's license is at stake. Using a transporter is not allowed by state law to help follow or retrieve dead or wounded game and is not allowed to lend a rifle to a hunter.

On a transported hunt, preparation of the meat and the trophy is the hunter's responsibility, though the hunter has the full complement of the boat's equipment at his disposal, including freezers, rigging and a hose to wash the blood off the deck.

Another aspect of hunting Alaska that hunters from other states may not know about is the prohibition against using radios to assist a hunter in the stalk. Radio traffic is monitored by the state game enforcement agencies. Most transport companies and guides do use radios to keep track of parties and prevent emergency situations.

# ONE GREAT BOAT HUNT

In the spring of 2006, I arranged with a transport company, Ninilchik Charters, operating out of Ninilchik and Seward, for a hunt in Prince William Sound.

The black bear is the undisputed king of Prince William Sound. His domain, the Chugach National Forest, is a steep, craggy land, rich with fir trees and rivers so precipitous they run in white ribbons down the black cliffs. The underbrush grows thick with huckleberries on the sidehills and salmonberry along the creeks. Moss hangs heavy in the trees and carpets the forest floor. Ideal conditions for black bear.

In June, daylight runs almost round the clock. We hunted the first evening until 11:30. I tried a stalk on the third bear I saw that evening. When I was within 50 yards (45.5 m) in the alders, it stopped feeding and began to clack its teeth in warning. Because I couldn't see it and it held the advantage of the high ground, I let it have the hill. When I returned to the boat that evening, we compared notes. Between eight of us, we'd seen sixteen bears.

The first bear of the trip was taken the next morning. A 5-foot (1.5 m) boar (measured from nose to tail), it had a beautiful, un-rubbed black pelt.

On one morning hunt, we waited along a beach within a bay fed by two glaciers. Every hour, one of the massive ice flows would "calve," giving birth to an iceberg with a crash that shook the bay like a sonic boom. Thousands of icebergs floated in the bay and migrated out into the passage, some as small as a coffee table, others as big as a house.

On the third day, Captain Bob Stumpff ran me in a skiff into a narrow bay. I waded to shore and found a place to wait with the wind in my face. For two hours I battled no-see-ums and mosquitoes. Then a bear padded out of the alders onto the tidal flat. A big boar, his long black hair rippled over powerful muscles as he grazed on the rich green grass. The water was rising fast and it cut me off from stalking closer. I laid down, held high on the shot and, when the smoke cleared, the bear had vanished into the brush. The next morning, at low tide, we moved in to find the trail and were unable to locate the bear after a long search.

Two days later, I spotted another bear at the shoreline, feeding on kelp and assorted goodies brought in on the tide. My Bushnell Elite rangefinder pegged him at 256 yards (233 m), but Ol' Blackie was too far to try a shot with the muzzleloader. He vanished into the woods.

Bear number six was a younger boar on a lonely beach. I spotted him at over a mile (1.6 km) and made the stalk only to see him disappear into the alders, still over 400 yards (364 m) away.

At the end of it, I packed my halibut catch and a sack of the biggest shrimp I've ever seen into a meat box, but didn't have any bear meat. Alaska haunts me still. The images of big boars prowling the shoreline will be burned in my memory as long as the black bear is king on the rocky ridges and in the icy canyons of Prince William Sound.

Alaska's boat-based bear hunts take place in May and June. Bears may be found on the beach or feeding below the snowline.

Chad Schearer (above), on a boat-based hunt, proves that it's possible to close the distance on a feeding bear. Patience pays off as he gets up close and personal.

Author Gary Lewis (right) in Alaska's Prince William Sound. For five days, base camp was a boat. Hunters took the inflatable skiff to the shore or cruised the banks in search of bear.

# BEAR BAITING

Many people, hunters included, have been conditioned to think that hunting bear over bait is unfair, that the hunter has an unsporting advantage. But contrary to what politicians and the media would have us believe, bait-hunting for bear is far from easy. Not all bears come to a bait. Some are naturally more suspicious. Some are afraid of other bears. Some guard the bait and hang around for hours, staying just out of sight during shooting light and feeding only at night.

The bait station provides the hunter with a higher percentage chance of seeing bear and it may give the opportunity to see more bears and evaluate the bear for trophy quality. The hunter has an opportunity to ensure that the bear is not a sow with cubs and the setup provides a better chance for precise shot placement.

Wildlife management agencies in bear country have regulations to control bear baiting. It is defined differently in various places and some states and provinces have outlawed it entirely. Know in advance what you can do and what you cannot do. Some states require that bait hunters are specially trained or licensed. Warning signs are often required.

When hunting black bear at any time of the season, remember it's all about the feed. You look for bears in the spring where the feed is concentrated in grassy openings in the valleys and on the hillsides. When the snow recedes, winter-killed elk and deer draw bears from miles around as the scent of rotting flesh and the raucous crows and ravens proclaim what's for dinner. Summer time finds bears in the berry patches. In the fall, the bears may try to intercept a herd of caribou, elk or blacktail deer on their annual migration.

In areas where baiting is illegal, it is a common and accepted practice to hunt over the gut piles of legally-taken deer and elk in hopes of seeing a bear. When fall salmon have spawned and died, the rotting flesh brings in bear from miles (kilometers) around. The best hunting spots are where the feed is concentrated.

Hunting over natural "baits" is an effective and sporting way to take a bear at any time during the season. But there are times and places where food is not concentrated. The hunter who makes his own concentrations of feed by bringing in bait is banking on Old Blackie's propensity for sniffing out a free meal.

This bait barrel is positioned, with deadfall arranged around it, so that the bear will present a good, broadside shot.

On a steady breeze, a bear can smell a meal at distances up to 3 miles (4.8 km), according to one California study.

Ray Crow (left) and Brian Bachman of Arrowhead Wilderness Lodge, with a Minnesota black bear Ray bagged with his muzzleloader.

## Timing

Brian Bachman is the owner of Arrowhead Wilderness Lodge. His company guides hunters from all over the world to their chance at a Minnesota bruin. He outfits for an average of forty hunters over two five-day periods and plans to be finished with his bear hunts each year prior to the start of grouse season when the bird hunters take to the woods.

Approximately two weeks before the season opener, Bachman begins setting out his baits on old sites and a few new ones each year. Most of his hunting takes place on public land or timber company property. For Bachman and his guides, morning is time to check the bait. Bachman's hunters hunt evenings only.

Bachman only hunts the fall seasons, but he had some advice about springtime baiting. Chances of getting a boar are higher in the spring. In the spring seasons, males are looking for the females and they're not afraid to come into the baits during the day. Sometimes a bigger bear stakes out a bait and defend it against all others. In this situation, Bachman recommends setting up a new bait nearby, where the other bears will find it in a couple of days.

A bear's home range may be anything from 1 or 2 square miles (1 to 3.2 sq km) to over 100 miles (160 km). In any given area, there may be a number of boars, single sows and sows with cubs. Early in the spring, there may be a single animal or a dozen that hit the site as they come out of hibernation. When the rut begins, in late May, the bigger boars begin to roam and the chance of seeing a bigger bear increases.

Temperature and conditions have a lot to do with the proper timing. In years with higher snow pack, the bears may emerge from their dens later in the spring. One year, the hunter finds tracks as early as late-March and another year, the bears may not show until mid-April. When to bait is often governed by specific regulation.

If I could choose only one time of day to sit a bait, I'd pick the evening hours. I'd hit the stand sometime in the early afternoon and wait it out until dark. But bears do come to the bait in the morning and may show up at any time of day. Bears are often surprised by hunters who show up at noon with a new load of goodies.

Ohio resident Jerry Baumbauer shot this bear on a boat-based hunt in Prince William Sound. This boar was feeding close to a snow-line when Jerry first spotted it.

## Location

The key to bait location is the travel corridor. Bears favor forest ground with a high moisture content. Timber is important for shade and escape cover. Find tracks and scat in this kind of cover and locate a bait site in proximity to accessible and abundant feed such as cropland or farms with fruit trees.

Use a topographical map and aerial photos to locate streams and crossings and timbered swamplands that give bear shade and cover. Travel corridors along valleys and ridges provide the clues to help you locate the site. Count on the prevailing wind to carry the scent to bears a mile (1.6 km) or more away. Try to set up between natural foods and bedding areas.

The landscape changes year after year. In years when there is a lot of natural food available, the bears come to the baits less frequently. When the oak trees are producing a lot of mast, the bears are less predictable. Bachman's area doesn't have a lot of oaks. The black bears he hunts are dependent on berries which are available for only a short time each year.

Set up fairly close to trails because you'll be carrying lots of food in to a site over the course of the season and hopefully carrying out a 200- to 300-pound (60 to 135 kg) bear. Mark the bait sites on a detailed map and set as a waypoint on a GPS unit to help locate the bait again when the light is low or weather has changed the landscape.

Bachman sets his stands 20 yards (18.2 m) from the baits to give his clients the best opportunity. The places he picks for stands are deep, dark and moist in heavy timber.

Natural baits, such as this cow elk carcass, attract bears very efficiently.

## Best Baits

Meat has long been a favorite bear attractant. Livestock carcasses left out in bear country bring in a hungry bear in less than a couple of days. Some hunters save bacon grease, while others make friends with restaurant owners and cart off the hamburger grease in 10-gallon (37.8 l) buckets. Where legal, a beaver carcass hung in a tree gives off the kind of strong odor that brings in a bear. Of course, bear love to eat fish. Any kind will do—salmon, suckers, carp and bream have all been used to bring bear to a bait site.

Apples, plums and peaches are in abundance in the fall in orchard country and bears don't care if the fruit has worms or bruises. Most orchard owners are happy to let bear hunters have some cast-off fruit with an eye toward removing a bear or two from the local population. Stale pastry, week-old bread and cookies are a good way to round out a bait site and add bulk to a bear's diet.

Pour bacon or fry grease around the bait bucket. Bears step in the mess and leave a trail that other bears follow right back to the bait site.

Brian Bachman prefers candy to all other baits. Since he started in 1978 he's used just about everything. Now he uses a clean, convenient and easy bait that is pleasant to be around—salted nut roll with peanuts and nougat. He buys it in 50-pound (22.5 kg) blocks. In fact, hunters eat a lot of it themselves while waiting in tree stands.

"I've had as many as a dozen bears working one bait," Bachman said. "We typically don't hunt a bait again that season after we've killed a bear there. We're taking about ten percent of the bears that we're feeding."

Bachman also made the point that bears remember a place where they got a meal. A bear will come back up to three more years after finding a bait there once.

## The Setup

Most hunters run three or more bait locations, to allow for flexibility in case one bait isn't drawing animals or another hunter stumbles on the site and camps out on it. The bait setup can be as simple as a 50-gallon (190 l) drum filled with donuts or as complex as a log crib built to channel movement and position the bear for a high-percentage, quartering-away bowshot. If a barrel is used, chain it to a tree or a log, to keep a hungry bear from rolling it away. Cut a 6- to 8-inch (15 to 20 cm) hole in the bottom to allow the bear to dig out a little food at a time.

Branches and deadfall arranged to position the bait and the bear. Note the trail camera on the tree to show the hunter when the bait is seeing the most activity.

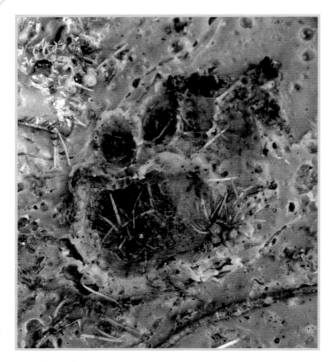

One bait hunter's tactic is to employ bacon grease around the bait barrel. Feeding bears track the scent out and lay a trail for other bears to follow back in.

Some hunters employ a "bear ball" in addition to the other baits and scents. On a rope strung from a branch, the ball keeps the bear distracted while it swats or bites the hanging bait. The ball is constructed of chicken wire wrapped around rock candy, meat or pastry. Rainwater runs off the ball and puddles on the ground beneath it, keeping a scent in the ground that intrigues a hungry bruin and keeps bears interested between replenishing trips to the site.

Ground blinds are used, but a tree-stand is often the best choice to keep the hunter and scent above the site. For a bow-hunting setup, select a tree not much more than 20 yards (18.2 m) away. For a rifle or muzzleloader, set up between 20 and 50 yards (18.2 and 45.5 m) from the bait.

Bachman sets his ladder stands to keep the hunter in position for a high-percentage shot. He recommends a lower stand so that an archer's arrow or a muzzleloader's ball gets a chance to penetrate both lungs instead of just one when the angle is steep.

Most hunters begin baiting at least two weeks before the season. Often, several trips a week are required to restock and keep bears interested.

## Scent Control

Bears know that the food is brought by humans, but they don't want to be there when the human is nearby. One tactic that some hunters use is to bring the bait at the same time each day, drop the goodies and get out. The bear, hearing the bait delivery vehicle leave now assumes that the site is safe once again. The hunter, wearing rubber boots, returns, then climbs the tree into the stand and waits.

Keep clothing and boots as scent-free as possible. Determine where the bear is most likely to make its approach then walk in on a different trail. Count on the prevailing wind to carry the scent into bear habitat. Position the tree stand to keep the pool of human scent away from the bait.

A tree at the bait site. Note the claw marks in the bark.

Bachman takes a different view of scent control: "I try to put as much human scent in there as I can. You're not going to fool them so I don't try to. If the clients want to come with me, I let them. The bears know there's activity there and they tolerate it. They're used to my scent and so I have a lot better success rate. The longer you sit on a bait, your chances go up every day. The bear are on alert when they get there. They do smell people. If there's a movement or a noise it will spook them."

## The Approach

When a bear is moving in to a bait site, it will probably come in slowly and cautiously. It may not be the biggest bear around, so it is on the alert to avoid a beating or worse. Its approach may alert other animals. Birds may stop singing, or suddenly fly off at the presence of the predator. Squirrels may go silent or bark their warning.

The bear will probably follow a trail through the deepest shade. Sometimes its presence is announced by the snap of a twig, but more often, just by a deepening shadow.

Kent Couch (right) used a .338 Winchester Magnum to take this big, coastal bear. Jerry Mitch's choice in a hand cannon is a .454 Casull.

# SCENTS AND LURES

A bear's most powerful sense is his sense of smell. More sensitive than the nose of the best bloodhound, a bear's olfactory organ allows him to follow the aroma of food or the odor of a sow in heat for miles (km). Scents and lures enable the hunter to enhance baits or, in the absence of a bait, to lure bear to the prospect of a meal or a procreation opportunity.

Fox or skunk urine, apples, dirt and a host of other smells have been developed to cover the human scent. Employ them on clothing or post on cotton balls located around a stand. When used in volume, the attractant scents can be enough to bring normally reluctant bruins on the prowl.

Scents and lures come in gels, spray bottles, gravy and as powder (just add water). Effective food scents include anise, apple, bacon, beaver castor, hickory smoke, corn, honey, watermelon, cherry, shellfish, and a variety of berries. When using attractant scents:
- Keep scents separated
- Set up to allow prevailing wind to carry scent toward bedding habitat
- Spray scent around bait from ground level to as high as ten feet
- Hang bait balls, sponges, or scent rags surrounding the stand
- Spray scent onto trails to allow bears to track scent away and give other bears a path to follow
- Freshen scent each time a bait is renewed so that bears associate the smell with fresh food
- Don't step in the scent or you'll run the risk of luring the bears into your stand or your truck
- Some attractants can repel bears if too much is used at one time

Be careful when using food scents and sow-in-heat lures, because the bear is expecting a meal or amorous relations. And it can be difficult to persuade Ol' Blackie otherwise, once his nose has told him what to expect at the end of the trail.

A bear on the box. Note the antennas on the collars. Houndsmen keep track of their dogs with telemetry, keeping better track of each animal during the chase.

## BAYING BEAR WITH HOUNDS

Whether you strike the trail in the rain forest or over on the dry side, a bear hunt with hounds may be the most exciting hunt of your life. That first surge of adrenaline when the dogs take the trail is only surpassed by the heady lonesome howl that means the dogs are close to the bear and that bark that means the bruin is treed or cornered on some windswept point. You may be following on foot, or mounted on a sure-footed mule, but you'd better get there fast.

Hunting with hounds has been maligned as unsporting by anti-hunting groups and by some hunters who should know better. It is neither a sure thing nor an easy thing to bring a bear to the point where he'll seek the refuge of a tree or a cave or stand and fight. The chase may take less than an hour, but more likely it will last the better part of a day. Some epic chases have lasted more than two days.

### The Dogs

Mike Martell hails from the state of Oregon, where hunting with hounds for black bear has been outlawed since 1994. Since that time, he has continued to hunt in places like California and British Columbia. A meticulous record keeper, he has treed more than 1,000 bears since he began bear hunting as a young man. For Mike, the hunt is about the adventure, the pursuit, the chess match and the struggle of man against beast. It is all these things, but mostly it is about the dogs. In over 30 years of hunting, he has developed some very definite ideas about what makes a good bear dog.

He started off hunting with German-bred Plott hounds and he still has a soft spot for the breed. "These dogs taught me how to catch a bear," he said. "As a net result I started to become more regimented and a little more focused and started to see that genetics played a key role in a big game dog.

There's no sound quite like the music of a hound baying "treed." To the houndsman, the bear hunt is all about the dogs.

"I'm a firm believer that on the dam and the sire's sides you have to go back three generations to have high expectations and high results. I'm not talking coon or bobcat or cougar dogs, I'm talking about a dog that is built to run for bear, that is big enough and strong enough to take some punishment. You need a dog that is determined and will stay with the hunt, even when the going gets tough." He's also found that the best bear dogs make very good raccoon, bobcat and cougar dogs.

There are several breeds of dogs that are used for hunting bear, but not every dog in every breed makes the grade. Just as a stable nag is not going to win the Triple Crown, not every hound rises to the level of a good bear dog.

"I began to find myself hunting an athletic type of bear. In one area we hunted, there were a lot of smart, old bears that were real runners, athletic bear that really gave the dogs a run for the money. In the 1980s, I started getting acquainted with Treeing Walker Coonhounds. They have the thoroughbred speed, the teeth and the physical ability to run over an extended period of time, catch the quarry and

make it climb. If the bear doesn't climb, the dog will grab the bear and make it sit or climb. Many breeds are used. Some of the best include the Plott hound, the Treeing Walker Coonhound, the Blue Tick hound and the Redbone hound.

"I believe in quality rather than quantity," Martell said. "I've treed more bears with two-dog and three-dog packs than with larger packs."

Martell works with several other houndsmen to keep dogs circulating in the same genetic profile. "If you know the makeup of the dog you can work around the deficiencies," Martell said. "Like a racehorse is geared just for the track and not for roping, a big game hound is a specialized animal that will ignore other game."

Martell also has definite ideas about the attitude of the hunter. "A dog wants to know what it can expect from its master. If its master is lazy, the dog knows it doesn't have to work as hard, because its master won't be there to back him up. But your dog will go in and fight for you, if you're willing to fight for him."

## The Gear

Technology has allowed houndsmen to become better at what they do and made the sport safer for the dogs. Telemetry equipment allows the hunter to monitor the location of each of his hounds and determine how the chase is going and where it's headed. If the bear is leading the dogs onto private land or into an unsafe area, the handler can make a decision more quickly, based on the input relayed by the electronics.

Each dog is fitted with a tracking collar and each collar is assigned a specific frequency. Each collar is equipped with a battery unit that allows up to 16,000 hours of usage. A circuit board inside the collar sends a beeping sequence back to the tracking unit. Collars can be fitted with an optional so-called treeing switch that is activated when the dog is looking up for more than three seconds.

The receiver permits the hunter to hear the transmission or signal from each individual dog. The handler slowly swings a hand-held directional antenna in a circle to determine in which direction the best signal is coming from. A dash-mounted GPS unit allows the hunter to chart the travel of the truck through an area and mark waypoints on bear trails. Hunters may also remove the GPS and take it into the woods when the dogs are barking treed. Finding the truck again on the way out is a matter of backtracking to the waypoint set in the parking area.

The last bit of electronics necessary to the bear hunt with hounds is a set of handheld radios. When there are dogs to catch or a bear to skin or a truck to find, it helps to communicate with every member of the party.

## The Rig Box

One of the most important pieces of hunting equipment that a houndsman owns is the rig box. Whether it is home-built or a production model, it must house the dogs in comfort during cold weather, yet provide enough air flow during the warm season that dogs don't die of heat stroke.

The box should ride inside the back of the pickup with enough room on each side to allow for the opening of the doors and for dogs to move inside

These hounds are leashed to trees to keep them back while the hunters move in with gun or camera.

On tether on the dog box. Each dog is trained to be a strike dog and each learns from the other. The small pack size allows the houndsman more flexibility and the dogs better interaction with their master.

of the bed below the rails. The rig box is subject to the worst kind of treatment that weather can throw at a vehicle. Plywood boxes work great for awhile, but do begin to warp and rot over time. Diamond plate or polycarbonate boxes last quite a bit longer.

If the rig box is built with a little forward thinking, it can be used to store guns, telemetry equipment, dog food, lead ropes and other supplies above the dog compartments. On top, the rig box should have tie-downs to allow for up to at least three leashed dogs to share the roof. Each compartment must be lockable to prevent a thief from stealing or damaging dogs and gear.

Lastly, the rig box should be washable. It helps to have a tip-up lid or removable kennels so that they can be aired out and hosed down from time to time to prevent transfer of bacteria and disease.

## Striking the Track

"Hunt early in the morning," Martell recommends. "That way, if you hit a trail sometime in the first six hours, you've got time for at least a four-hour chase before dark." But if you hunt long enough, you'll probably get a chance to spend the night in the woods a few times over the seasons.

The strike might be within the first minutes or the last hour of the hunt. If the track is cold, the dog gives a light bark and if the track is hot, the dog barks louder. And the chases generally last between one and four hours. "If you get into a six- or seven-hour chase, your odds of catching that bear drop off immensely," Martell warned.

To Martell, every dog has the ability to be a strike dog. He allows each dog to lead off the chase, rotating the honor so that each has the experience and confidence to take on a bear solo.

The dogs are rigged in a box that normally rides in the back of the pickup. In the hunt area, the handler snaps lead lines to the dog's collar, anchoring the dogs to the top of the rig box. They'll ride there until the smell of a bear is brought to them on the wind, then they bark so loudly, it sounds like they're going to blow the cab off the truck.

## The Chase

The bear could tree in the first five minutes or go for five more hours. Some bears just keep walking, leading the dogs on an easy chase that never ends in a tree. Other bears take off on a run that gives the dogs the workout of their lives.

At some point in the chase, the bear may decide to stand his ground. When the bear turns to face his pursuers, a dog could get hurt. Sometimes there will be a brief tussle then the bear hits the trail again. Other times, the bear decides to do all-out battle and he won't quit until every dog has been beaten or cowed.

Most races ultimately end with the bear going up a tree. The bear knows it is safe in the tree for awhile. The dogs can't reach it, though they try, often wearing the bark of the tree off in big patches, trying to reach the bear. Approach a treed bear with caution. When he sees a human, and if he sees an opening, he's likely to jump out of the tree and head off on another run before a shot can be taken.

And of course, the treed bear might not be what the hunter is after. It might be a small bear, or a sow with cubs. The hunter might be looking for a cinnamon or a blonde and turn down a bruin with a black pelt. Sometimes the hide is rubbed and the hunter turns it down in favor of a long-haired bear that is a better candidate.

A cinnamon-phase black bear in the limbs of a tree. Baying a bear gives the hunters a chance to evaluate each animal for trophy quality. Often, the dogs are leashed and the bear released to run another day.

One moment we were bouncing along the road in the truck and the next moment we struck a run-able bear track. The dogs went crazy on the rig box. They'd caught the fresh scent of a bear and he was close. Mark and Terry were hunting with Walker hounds and I was still running my Plotts; Shorty and Devil. Kizzy was a black and tan from Idaho that I'd started on raccoons and had proved to be a tough bay dog and a top tree dog.

Trouble was, my dogs couldn't keep up with the faster Walkers. I decided that after an hour or two, I'd relay my dogs into the race when the bear crossed a road. It worked out just that way. After two hours, I turned my dogs loose and we were listening to them go, driving along, keeping pace along the road.

Then the race took a turn and the dogs were below the road, just yards (meters) from where we'd parked the pickups. My son Mike was a little boy then and he'd brought along a camera and he told me he wanted to take a picture of the bear when it came into sight. But his nerve failed him. He handed me the camera and lit out for the truck when the brush started popping.

I snapped a picture as the bear hit the road then I turned and dived into the back of the pickup as the bear blasted into the bush on the other side of the road. My dogs were right on his tail. When the bear had gone, I looked up at little Mike and he said, "Dad, that bear scattered us like a flock of sheep. Didn't he?"

Across the road, the dogs brought the bear to bay at the edge of a small pond. Agitated now, he tried to climb a tree, but the dogs would just grab him and pull him back down. Once, the bear chased Devil and grabbed him. They went into the water, rolling over and over and came out fighting.

Not a single one of us had a gun, because we were just exercising the bears and this had started

# THE HATCHET BEAR

By Mike Martell as told to Gary Lewis

out like a typical race. Now the race was out of control. My dogs were the only ones left in the scrap. All the other dogs had had enough of this mean little bear. All he wanted to do was fight.

We started throwing rocks to break it up, or get him to run or go up a tree. After fifteen minutes, he gave up and took off on a dead run again, my dogs right behind him. I had the feeling we had pushed the bear past the point where he was interested in saving his own hide. He was madder than blazes and equipped to kill any of the dogs or one of us. I had to pull the dogs off and back away before it was too late.

Back in the pickup, I followed the sound of the hounds and kept up with them as they climbed the ridge. When I was even with them, I stopped to listen and heard them baying solid. The bear had stopped again and I was a little bit concerned. How was I going to catch the dogs and keep that bear from chewing on me?

The only thing I had for a weapon was a 26-inch (66 cm) double-bit cruising axe. I grabbed it, because after what I'd seen earlier, I didn't want to run into that bear empty-handed. He seemed like he'd rather stop and fight than turn and run.

It took me about ten minutes to reach the dogs. A big cedar blowdown was in the way and a dog stood on top of the log. I crawled under the log and took the time to peek around the corner. The bear stood there about 8 feet (2.4 m) away with the dogs in his face. Suddenly he winded me and broke, running up the creek bed with the dogs hot on his tail. I followed right behind the dogs, going as fast as I could.

Again the bear stopped and turned to fight. He looked us over as the dogs closed in, showing no fear. He'd had enough.

The first dog he caught was Devil. He grabbed him with his jaws, then shook him and swung him even as the other dogs dove in to the fight. Devil went flying 10 feet (3 m) into the air when the bear let go.

The bear caught Shorty next, shook him like a rag doll then slung him aside and went for Kizzy. He rolled Kizzy over in the dirt, bit her and threw her aside. My dogs were battered, but they tried to regroup. It looked like this bear had too much speed and agility for them. He was about to whip all of us, me included.

With no dogs now between us, the bear turned his total attention on me. He gave me that "You're next" look and started for me from about 30 feet (9 m) away. 25 feet (7.6 m). 20 feet (6 m). And I was thinking, "This bear won't take me, he'll break and run at the last second." 15 feet (4.6 m). I drew back the axe like a baseball player. 10 feet (3 m). He was coming at me at an angle, head down, mouth open, centered to take me at the thigh. 5 feet (1.5 m).

By the time his head was 3 feet (1 m) away, I swung with all I had.

The axe took the bear through the left eye, nose and face and buried into the skull all the way to the handle. But his momentum carried him into me and knocked me backwards into the ground, flat on my back, pinned to the ground.

Because I was not sure whether I'd killed him or not, I scrambled up and backed away. He lay lifeless. I'd killed him with one blow to the head.

The dogs piled on and chewed him, taking out their frustrations for the beating they'd gotten.

I was standing there, looking down at the dead bear when Terry arrived. He just looked from the bear to the dogs to me and back at the bear again....

# GOING GUIDED

Outdoor shows are where many hunting guides book their new business for the year. You get there early on a Saturday, push your way through the crowd, look at the photos, run your fingers through the hair on a bear pelt and soon imagine yourself still-hunting down some forest trail in the north.

Will it be everything you imagined it to be? There are steps you can take to ensure that your trip across the state or across the country will be successful.

Decide first who you want to spend all that time with. What can you expect from your regular partners? Are they the kind of people who keep their spirits up when the rain falls for four days straight and much of your time is spent trying to keep dry? You should only hunt with people with similar expectations.

Be equally careful with who you book. Ultimate success is not guaranteed. You are still subject to the same variables you experience closer to home. It could rain the whole time and blow out all the rivers, or an unseasonable snowstorm might drive the animals to lower elevations. Be careful if the outfitter assures you that you will bag your bear. Real life does not always work that way.

Contact the Fish and Wildlife department in the state or province where you intend to hunt. Ask if outfitters and guides in that state or province are required to hold licenses. Is your outfitter's license current? Be aware, some state laws say that hunters using the services of an unlicensed outfitter or guide may be held in violation.

Eight months later you board a plane. You have invested more cash than your family thinks you have and you are excited. Will it be everything you imagined it to be? Too often, a well-polished smile, a colorful display, some bear skulls, long-haired rugs and a few full-color photos are enough to convince us to part from our money.

## Referrals

If the outfitter is worth the money, there will be a list of clients who've hunted with them. And there will be a list of folks who will give a good recommendation. Of course, those former clients should get a phone call, but the best referrals aren't on the list at all.

Ask for the names and contact information of the clients who went home empty-handed. Find out why, but remember there are two sides to every story. To be fair, some clients are simply not equipped for success, due to unrealistic expectations or other self-imposed limitations. Ask the reference about the guide's ethics, and if they would book a trip with that outfitter again.

Go on-line and find out what other hunters have to say. Organizations such as The Hunting Report, Safari Club International, and the North American Hunting Club, among others, keep files on outfitters.

You can be more confident if you ask the right questions in advance.

Even very cold and icy water won't deter a black bear from its journey.

On a guided hunt in Alaska or Canada, a floatplane (above) may be used to give the hunters access to roadless areas in country seen by only a handful of hunters each year. Finding bears in trees (left) becomes an added challenge on any hunt.

Matt and Dara Smith hunted with Dan Syfert from Wapiti Archery Outfitters to take this nice bear in southwest Oregon. Experienced guides know their areas far better than the average hunter can hope to in many years of hunting. A successful guided trip, in the long run, may be less expensive than a series of do-it-yourself hunts.

## What to Expect

Every hunt is different. Want to know what to expect? Make sure you ask as many questions as possible beforehand.

License and tag fees are probably not included in the price of the hunt. Air travel from your home to the jumping-off point is probably not included, but the price of float plane travel may be. Find out in advance. Ask the outfitter what you should expect of him and his crew and assure him what he can expect of you. Will you be expected to haul water, chop wood or feed the horses? How will the hunt be conducted? Does the guide use spot and stalk methods or will he put you on a stand in the morning and come pick you up again after dark? Will the guide butcher and pack out your animal?

Ask also about the previous year. A client has the right to know if a severe drought or a hard winter took a toll on wildlife.

Meals are often included in the price of the hunt, but some outfitters have opted to exclude food as a way to keep prices down. Food can make or break the experience. If it's hard for you to live without a big breakfast or steak and seafood every night, let the outfitter know about it in advance. If money is tight, the cook might be forced to make sandwiches with bologna and processed cheese. If you can't stand that kind of fare, make sure the outfitter knows about it in advance. And if it's imperative that there be chocolate bars or a half-dozen cookies in the lunch sack, you can bring them yourself.

The outfitter and guide want to see every hunt end with the client having had at least an opportunity to tag a bear. The reality of hunting is that not every hunter does it right. An opportunity is all a client can reasonably expect.

The guide expects the hunter to have done at least a little bit of research about the animal and its tendencies, habits and habitat.

A guide's biggest disappointment is the client who didn't have the self-discipline in the months before the hunt to get in shape. I once watched a hunter stop a stalk when he was 150 yards (136.5 m) from the bear because he just couldn't walk any farther. That bear walked away and the hunter never had another chance.

This out-of-state hunter takes a rest to make the shot across the canyon. Practice under field conditions and shoot at different distances to prepare for the situations that may be encountered on a guided hunt.

On a western spot-and-stalk hunt, there might be miles (kilometers) to cover on foot. The stalk might come in the last hour of light with a slope to descend and another to climb before a shot is made. And when the hunt is with hounds and the bear is treed, there may only be a few minutes to get from point A to point B before the bear decides to go head-to-head with the dogs.

Start walking or jogging at least three times a week. Go to the gym. Climb the stairs at work instead of taking the elevator. Get a personal trainer. Do whatever it takes, but lose the weight and gain the lung capacity to go that last 150 yards (136.5 m). Get in good physical shape and make sure you are bringing the right gear for the weather that might be encountered. Practice shooting under the conditions and at the distances you will encounter in the field. When you finally arrive at your destination, go at it with all the enthusiasm you can muster.

In my experience, most hunters go over-gunned. Make sure you can shoot whatever you bring and shoot it well. The best guides require that you shoot first before they take you on a hunt. Be prepared or be prepared to be embarrassed if you can't put three bullets in a 5-inch (12.7 cm) circle at 100 yards (91 m).

On the hunt, if there are support personnel involved, such as guides, cooks and deckhands, it doesn't hurt to tip a little in advance of the final gratuity. The crew can get burnt out toward the end of a long season and a little attitude adjustment in the form of some folding money, cheerful smiles and a charitable demeanor on your part go a long way toward making the trip a good one.

Be cheerful, stay out all day and listen to your guide. You paid him your hard-earned money to make your stay worthwhile. The attitude you take will help create the memories you bring home.

# CHAPTER FOUR

# Gear

**B**ear hunting equipment is specialized to fit the individual needs of the hunter, the habitat and style of hunting. Since bears are most likely to be spotted in low light situations, the hunt requires big glass with polished and coated lenses for the best light transmission. Because the biggest animals can absorb a lot of punishment and keep going, rifles, cartridge combinations and muzzleloading and archery tackle should be chosen with care. Proper equipment, combined with good scouting technique and paying attention to detail on the hunt will help the hunter bring home the bear. Season after season.

## OPTICS

When the wind changed, the rain stopped. But on southeast Alaska's Prince of Wales Island, the rain seldom stops for long. I fired up the rented Dodge and went hunting. Soon it was raining again.

After two days of driving rocky roads, walking beaches, slogging through miles of muskeg and countless clearcuts, I had seen two bears. One was a juvenile inside city limits. The other was a massive boar that prowled the beach across the bay from Fireweed Lodge in Klawock. Through binoculars, we watched him turning over boulders, eating the knee-high grass, and nibbling new buds from shore-side saplings.

Good optics allowed me to judge the size of the bear and the quality of the hide. Distance viewing allows you to see the bear first, and a good riflescope puts you on target.

Black bear hunting is about selection. As with all hunting you have to know your game and your intended target. That requires good vision. And because it is so difficult to get close to bears, long-range viewing is critical. Quality optics are an essential part of your kit.

Nathan Endicott glassing mountainsides for foraging bears. A bear hunt is a great time to bring a young hunter along. Warming winds blow in the canyons, the wildflowers are in bloom and newborn fawns wobble alongside their mothers.

## Binoculars

For light transmission, field of view and portability in the field, the best binocular for the bear hunter is a full-size porro prism model with a 7x to 8x magnification and 35 mm to 50 mm objective lens. The porro prism models have an offset or dogleg shape. These provide a wider field of view than roof prism models which have the straight shape. Large, multi-coated objective lenses provide superior light transmission. Bear country is not the place for compact binoculars. You may spend hours behind the glasses, watching for animals on the opposite hillside. Compacts just don't give the resolution, clarity, and ability to see in low light that full-size models provide.

Rubber armored, waterproof binoculars are essential when hunting bear. Rainstorms can blow in without warning. You'll just have to pull the hat down low over your eyes and keep looking. There's a bear out there somewhere. If your binoculars fog up because moisture finds its way inside, it may be days before the glasses are clear once again.

Don't handicap yourself by carrying your binoculars in your backpack. Binoculars should be quickly accessible. To minimize back and neck strain, use a strap system that puts the weight on the shoulders.

## Spotting Scopes

For a closer look at a bear, a spotting scope is often necessary. I use a variable-zoom Alpen scope that allows me to change the magnification from 18x to 36x.

You want the best spotting scope you can afford, because you will spend a lot of time using it. Low quality glass will give you a headache and may reduce the time you can spend searching for a bear. If possible, take your top three choices outside of the store and focus on some small distant object. Whichever scope renders the subject with the most clarity and color is the scope to pick.

In the field, you may have the opportunity to look at several bears before finding the one you pursue. Zooming in close to watch a small bruin, or a sow with cubs feeding across a hillside is a treat by itself, and makes the trip worthwhile.

## Laser Rangefinders

For the bear hunter, one of the best optics developments is the laser rangefinder. On a hunt in unfamiliar terrain it is very difficult to estimate range with any degree of reliability. The best that two hunters could do before the rangefinder came along was for each to estimate the distance, compare estimates and then agree on a number in between. With a rangefinder, the guesswork is gone. All that remains is to know the ballistics of the rifle and cartridge combination.

Some rangefinders are integrated with binoculars. Most are a monocular that functions without readout until activated by depressing the trigger button one time. It is ready to "shoot" the range when the display lights up in the viewfinder. Simply align the aperture on the target and press the button again.

I carry a Bushnell Elite 1500. This model has several modes that allow viewing in the rain and through the brush without getting inadvertent readings. It operates on a 9-volt battery and has an adjustable twist-up eyepiece to adjust for distance from the eye for eyeglass wearers.

This segment of the market is new, but the technology is current and all the major brands have high quality offerings. Some models have longer-range capability. Match the rangefinder to the real estate where you hunt. Decide what you can afford and compare several models side by side.

For the spot-and-stalk hunter, in wet or dry country, a spotting scope can mean the difference between seeing bears and not seeing them. A variable scope is the most useful, because it allows the hunter the ability to scan large areas then zoom in for a closer look.

Author Gary Lewis used a scope on his muzzleloader for this hunt, and used a range finder to make sure the distances were right. The range finder takes all the guesswork out of judging distance. On what might be a once-in-a-lifetime hunt, a range finder can make the difference.

Lee Van Tassell with a big bear that fell to a .338 Winchester Magnum and a 250-grain Nosler Partition. Lee favors a 3-9x Leupold compact scope and keeps it dialed at low range unless he needs to make a long shot.

## Riflescopes

A riflescope should be rugged enough to take the kind of abuse that can happen in rough, rocky country. It should not be prone to fogging. Spring storms can bring enough rain to fog cheaper optics. Make sure the riflescope is waterproof.

On a short-range rifle like a .30-30 or a .45-70, a two-power scope is a good choice. Shots will be at close range and the wide field of view afforded by the low power scope allows the hunter to find the target quickly.

For longer range, the four-power is adequate for shots out to 300 yards (273 m). The four-power is simple. With it, there is never the chance that the scope will be set on a higher magnification when the shot must be taken at close range.

The problem with using higher power in your scope is that it reduces the field of view. Field of view is the expanse of the subject within the field of the optical circle. As magnification is increased, the field of view diminishes. I have talked to many hunters who, when given a close range opportunity, could not find the animal in the scope they had left dialed in at the maximum power. It is easier to find the target quickly in the scope when field of view is larger.

Reticles vary from a simple post with an aiming dot to military style mil-dots allowing the scope to be used as a range-finder. Plain crosshairs are fine but a duplex style crosshair is my choice on a hunting scope because the outer portion of each crosshair is very thick, tapering to a thin, aiming intersection. This configuration allows your eye to go quickly to the center of the scope.

The most important light transmitting feature is the size of the objective lens. The cone of light projected from the rear of the scope should coincide with the diameter of the eye's pupil at low light. This is measured by arriving at what is known as the "exit pupil," a measurement of the diameter of the tiny circle of light in the eye lens where the image is focused. It should be between 5 mm and 7 mm. This is computed by dividing the objective diameter by the scope's magnification. So a 32 mm objective with 4x magnification has an exit pupil of 8 mm. A 40 mm objective with 8x magnification has an exit pupil of 5 mm.

Be more concerned with lens quality than lens size. Good optics have coated lenses. The coating reduces reflection and enhances the passage of light, improving the clarity of what the hunter can see through the scope.

Choose the scope that is best for the type of hunting you intend to use it for and use the best quality rings and mounts to make it a part of your rifle. And spend whatever time and ammunition it takes to learn how the rifle/scope/cartridge combination performs at different distances.

# RIFLES AND BULLETS

Some hunters have been known to dismiss the black bear as an animal easily dispatched with any rifle that may be at hand. Limited experience with bears that have been taken quickly has led some to conclude that bears are easy to kill. In my opinion, it's a dangerous attitude to adopt when the animal may measure over 7 feet (2 m) from nose to tail and weigh 600 pounds (270 kg)! No matter your level of hunting expertise and experience, it would be unwise to go into the field under-gunned.

Neither should a bear hunter carry too much gun. I've met plenty of people who hunted with a rifle that they were afraid to shoot.

## Equipped for Bear

Bears are tough. A mortal wound seldom puts one down on the spot. Use a bullet that will break bone and do tissue damage and leave a hole large enough that the bear continues to bleed.

The hunter who needs a rifle for pursuing bear specifically should know that, while even the .22 centerfires are legal for bear in some states, the best choice is a bigger caliber. Bear run when shot and their long hair can soak up a lot of blood. Quite simply, bigger bullets make bigger holes and a good blood trail makes following the bear a lot easier.

Wood and blue versus synthetic and stainless. Let the environment dictate the choice. If hunting in a wet climate, a synthetic stock is hard to beat (left).

At this hunting camp, everyone unloads their firearms outdoors then stores ammo and guns (bolts open) in one room (above). This way, accidents are kept to a minimum.

Lee Van Tassell with a bear that fell to a 200-grain Nosler Ballistic Tip. This bear popped out of the brush onto a log skidder trail, less than ten paces away when the author spotted him. With the scope set on a low power, Lee was able to make a quick, killing front-on shot that dropped the bear in its tracks.

I consider the .270 Winchester to be the minimum caliber for the bear hunter. The .270 makes a fine deer rifle and a great antelope gun, but it doesn't sustain the energy required to consistently kill bear in spot-and-stalk or self-defense situations. Certainly, this bullet has accounted for a lot of bears over the years, but it is a marginal performer when it comes to breaking bone and putting a bear down for good.

For a dedicated bear gun, the .30-06 Springfield, loaded with a premium 180- or 200-grain bullet, is an excellent all-around choice for a black bear.

To bring more energy to the endeavor, step up to a .300 Winchester Magnum. You want to hit the bear so hard that it goes down and stays down. The .325 Winchester Short Magnum, 8mm Remington Magnum, the .338 Winchester Magnum, the .350 Remington Magnum, the .35 Whelen and .375 H&H Magnum are great for reaching the vitals and putting an animal down in a hurry. If you have to track the bear, it will likely be bleeding out of an entrance and an exit wound.

For close-range stalking, like you'll find on the beaches of Alaska or when hunting over bait, consider using a .45-70. This old military cartridge, and its cousin, the 450 Marlin, are close to the perfect close-quarters choice when loaded with a .300-grain Nosler Partition Protected Point or similar bullet.

It is also important to have a well-constructed bullet. Use premium bullets such as the Nosler Partition or Accubond, Swift A-Frame or Scirocco, Hornady Interbond, Winchester Failsafe, Barnes Triple Shock or the Trophy Bonded.

## Practice

The most powerful rifle, the best optics and premium ammunition aren't worth a thing without the skill to place the bullet. It's like strapping on Air Jordans and hoping to hit the game-winning three-pointer without going to a practice. There's no doubt that there's pressure on the hunter to make a shot in front of the guide or one of your hunting partners.

Focus is the key to accuracy. Focus on the form, the breathing, the safety and trigger squeeze. Focus on one small crease behind the front shoulder. But that focus should begin months before the hunt, whether the hunt is in the hills behind the house or in another state.

Spend the first sessions shooting from a bench at the range. Sight-in, first at 25 yards (22.75 m), 50 yards (45.5 m) and 100 yards (91 m). Rest the gun on sandbags, pull the butt into your shoulder, and focus on the target. Move the safety switch from "safe" to "fire." Take a breath, let half of it out, hold and squeeze the trigger. Have a partner load the rifle, sometimes bolting the gun on an empty chamber. Such dry-firing practice can reveal flinching and can help correct it.

Then, as accuracy begins to show on paper, with clusters of neatly punched holes around the bulls-eye, move the targets to 200 yards and beyond. And keep track. I bring a ruler and measure the bullet drop at 100 (91 m), 200 (182 m), 300 (273 m), 400 (364 m) and 500 yards (455 m). The data, on a little strip of paper taped to the bell of my scope is an instant reference if I need to take a long shot.

Then leave the range behind and head out into the desert or the woods. Remembering your safety rules, look for a safe and legal place to shoot. Know your target and what's beyond it. Then practice shooting at extreme angles and anywhere from 50 yards out to 500 yards. Shoot from the prone position, kneeling and standing. If you're right-handed, shoot left-handed and vice versa.

To practice for a charging bear, set a target at 25 yards (22.75 m), 15 yards (13.7 m) and 5 yards (4.6 m). Shoot the far target first, engage the middle target next and the closest target last. Keep it up until you can hit each target as fast as you can cycle the action.

Make safety part of the routine and hone your focus on the target. Shoot at least once a month leading up to the season opener.

## Shot Placement

If at all possible, wait for a standing shot unless the idea of trailing a wounded bear into thick brush appeals to you. Every bear is different. When hit, some run away. Others attack. Don't let anybody fool you. A black bear can kill just as dead as a brown bear can. Whether using bow, rifle muzzleloader or handgun, go armed with a weapon you can shoot well.

There are seven good shots presented by the bear hunter. The easiest, and the one every hunter hopes to get, is the broadside shot.

• Broadside – Elk and deer hunters are conditioned to shoot game in the heart/lung area behind the shoulder. On a bear, this is a deadly shot as well, but you're likely to have to trail a bear shot through the lungs. Instead, aim a little ahead of the point of the shoulder to break the

Leave the scope set on the lowest power when moving from stand to stand. Bear hunts can end at close range. This bear was spotted working in the undergrowth. Lee used an elk call to make a distress sound. The bear came straight in.

Lee spotted this bear and another early in the morning entering a swamp. He chose the .45-70 with 300-grain Nosler Partitions for this hunt, because he knew it was going to be a close-range affair.

scapula. Hit a broadside bear through the scapula and the spinal cord, which lies between the scapulas, will be taken out. The bear will go down like a ton of bricks.

- Standing on back legs – With a bear on his back legs, center-punch it between the front legs. The bullet will take out the heart/lungs and break the spine, dropping it in its tracks.

- Quartering – With a bear that is quartering toward you, hold one-third to halfway up the body between the head and the shoulder to punch the projectile through the scapula and the heart and lungs.

- Quartering away – Because a bear's heart and lungs are protected between the front shoulders, the quartering away shot is the best bet for a bowhunter. With the bear quartering away, hold just behind the line of the front leg, one-third to halfway up the body, to put the arrow or bullet into the vitals.

- Head shot – Sometimes a head shot is all you get. From the side, put the bullet below the ear to take out the brain and put Mr. Big on the ground. From the front, break the bridge between the eyebrows. The neck is a hard one to shoot, because it's hard to break the spine without a perfectly placed shot, though, if the bear's head is up, this will put the bear down in a hurry.

- Head-on charge – This is the reason to have the riflescope dialed to the lowest setting. At 25 mph (40 kmph), that bear is coming fast. At high speed, it is hard to get the scope on the animal. Forget about saving the head for the taxidermist. Go center of body mass and start shooting. When a bear's head is up, hit it under the jaw. If there's time to aim, hold on the throat and drive the bullet back through the vitals. Sometimes a better option is to take the bear in the shoulder to break it down. Usually this shot gives you time for a second. Keep shooting until you're sure the bear is down for good.

- Going away – This is a hard shot to make, but it is very effective when the bullet is placed right, destroying the central nervous system and major skeletal components. Hit the bear at the top of the tail to break its pelvis and take its back legs out of the action.

# FACE-TO-FACE WITH A BLACK BEAR

Sometimes a boy wants to do his own laundry. There is probably a good explanation for coming home with bear excrement all over one's clothes. But it probably wouldn't explain the presence of certain other kinds of—ahem—evidence inside of one's garments.

I met a fellow, we'll call him Pete, and we naturally started talking about hunting and I showed him a picture of my daughter's first bear. Pete asked where we'd hunted and when I told him the name of the unit in northeast Oregon, he had a story to tell. "That's steep country," he said. "I hunted elk there one year and got run over by a bear."

Naturally, I wanted to hear more. "Did you get his license plate?"

When Pete says the country is steep, he isn't just a-woofin'. Those mountains that drain into the Minam, the Imnaha and the Snake are as steep as a cow's face and as rough as 80-grit sandpaper to a flea on roller skates.

It slopes deceptively easy up from the river bottoms then shoots for the sky all at once. And every step has a rock to roll under it and so many snakes you want to walk around on stilts.

Pete was moving slowly, side-hill, with his gun carried easy in his right hand. Not only did he have an elk tag, he also had a bear tag. And if there's one place in Oregon that has more bears than this northeast corner of the state, Pete hadn't heard about it. Three-quarters of the way up the hogback, he worked along a game trail, watching the country ahead. Ahead, an old pine tree was down and Pete walked around the root wad.

At the base of the root wad, dug out of the soft dirt that the tree had left, was a big, deep hole with fresh tracks going in and out. So many tracks, it looked like the road to church on Easter Sunday. Now if you've ever come upon a cave or a hole in the ground, you know that you don't pass such places by. You stop and look inside.

And if there are fresh tracks, your heart beats faster, because something big and hairy with sharp teeth might be waiting. Mostly, the tracks date back to the Pleistocene and the hole is empty. If you're lucky, you might find some hair or a quill or a fossil to tell you what kind of animal once made its home there.

Pete eased up to the hole and looked down inside. Right into the startled yellow eyes of a black bear. "I think he thought I was going to eat him," Pete said.

For a moment, the two predators faced off. The omnivore with his beady eyes and long, pearly fangs and the human with his big, round peepers and meat-chewing eyeteeth.

The bear made the first move. He swung his head and looked behind him, back inside the cave, as if he was looking for another way out. And I thought to myself, he doesn't have another way out.

That's when Pete stepped way back—to give him some space. Stepping backward off the mountain is a little like stepping off a cliff, except you don't fall quite as far. Pete lost four feet of elevation and dropped to eye level with the hole.

From the bear's point of view, where a moment before there'd been a hunter, now there was nothing but blue sky and freedom. And that bear came out of his hole as fast as a cat with his tail on fire doing what a bear does in the woods, leaving fresh steaming piles at 30 miles per hour (48 kmph). Right on top of the startled hunter.

When the bear cleared him, Pete let go of his rifle and rolled down the hill. For all he knew, he was being eaten. Getting that rifle back was priority number one. He scrambled uphill, clawing handfuls of dirt to get to his gun.

The bear stopped to take a look back, but now he'd seen enough. Pete grabbed his rifle, spun, rolled his shoulder into the dirt and found the bear in his scope, just as the animal disappeared around the corner of the hill. Gone.

When he stood up again and brushed himself off, Pete found the freshest sign he'd ever seen. The bear had been saving it up for some time too. "I had bear scat all the way from my feet up to my chest."

I didn't ask, but I'm thinking the bear wasn't the only one with a case of loose bowels.

Pete didn't get the bear's license plate, but he did get something even better. GPS coordinates. He says when he draws a spring bear tag for that unit, he's going back to find that cave. We hope he doesn't get taken to the cleaners again.

— Gary Lewis

Author Gary Lewis carried a CVA Kodiak Pro .50 (left) on this wet weather hunt. The stainless steel barrel and laminated stock resist rusting and warping which can cause accuracy problems when you don't need accuracy problems. With a muzzleloader (right), accuracy, to 100 yards, can be equal to that of all but the best centerfire rifles.

# BLACKPOWDER

A muzzleloader gives the hunter one chance to hit the target with a well-placed shot. It's an option that comes with the responsibility and the challenge to become a better hunter. And it's a choice that many bear hunters are making as muzzleloaders become more popular throughout North America.

In the fall, most bears are taken incidental to the hunt for other game. As hunters carry their muzzleloaders on special deer and elk seasons throughout the country, they may encounter a bear. And the rifle is pressed into action. Most muzzleloading rifles, when loaded with heavy, conical bullets, are up to the task.

Due to the nature of the load combinations typically used in muzzleloaders, the ballistics and energy of the bullet limit the effective shooting range of the muzzleloader to 150 yards (137 m) or less in most cases. For tree-stander hunters, this isn't a concern, but for those who would find their game in clear cuts or on the beach, it puts all the importance on the patience and stalking skill of the individual.

## Rifling

Muzzleloaders are rifled with different twists to ensure stabilization and accuracy of the bullet. Traditional side-lock percussion and flintlock guns are often rifled with a "slow" 1:66 turn for shooting patched round balls.

Many sidelock rifles are rifled to 1:48. This is a good twist for hunters who may choose to shoot either a patched round ball or a conical bullet.

Most new inline rifles come equipped with a 50-caliber barrel that has been given a fast 1:24 to 1:28 twist for the optimum stabilization of conical and saboted bullets.

## Take a Powder

A 50-caliber muzzleloader operates in the optimum range when used with blackpowder FFFg, Pyrodex (a cleaner-burning blackpowder substitute), Hodgdon Triple Seven, or one of several other blackpowder substitutes. Never use smokeless powder in your muzzleloader.

Conventional blackpowder has two drawbacks: It is more difficult to ship and transport blackpowder due to the legal ramifications of owning an explosive substance; and it is more difficult to clean than blackpowder substitutes. To clean the barrel, allow a little more time and use soap and hot water. In its favor, blackpowder ignites at 450 degrees and is a reliable choice when you're using a No. 11 percussion cap.

As interest grew for muzzleloading in the last few decades, Hodgon introduced their well-known Pyrodex as a safer, cleaner-burning alternative to blackpowder. Today, it is sold in loose-powder form or in pre-measured pellets.

In 2002, Hodgdon introduced a new product they named Triple Seven. This clean burning propellant leaves no corrosive sulfur in the barrel. Triple Seven is also available either in its loose powder form or in easy-to-use pellets. For the first-time muzzleloading hunter, two 50-grain Triple Seven pellets make loading and shooting the rifle safe and convenient. With Triple Seven, clean up is greatly simplified. Just use water and a patch on the end of the cleaning rod.

## Bullets for Big Game

I lean toward strong, heavy bullets when it comes to big game with sharp teeth and long claws. With a 50-caliber muzzleloader, for game up to and including black bear and elk, the 45-caliber, 260-grain Nosler Partition HG in a sabot is a good choice.

When you need close-range knockdown power, consider PowerBelt's 338-grain Aerotip or the 300-grain CVA Buckslayer. When you may encounter game at longer range, it's safe to load 120 grains of powder behind a bullet.

When it comes to food, black bears are creatures of opportunity. In the spring, the hunter can find them where the grass is green, on the mountain slides and in coastal flats like the one where Dudley McCarity found this bear. For the muzzleloading hunter, the challenge is to stalk within range and make one good shot.

Doug Jeanneret with his .50-caliber Knight rifle in preparation for a June bear hunt. An in-line muzzleloader, equipped with a scope, may not be the ballistic equivalent of a modern centerfire rifle, but at the terminal end, there's little difference. And the challenge of making one good shot with a big bullet adds excitement to an already exciting event.

## Loading and Shooting

Before loading the muzzleloader, confirm that it is not loaded already. Centerfire rifles and shotguns are easily checked by opening the breech. With a muzzleloader, you must use your ramrod. When you're completely sure that the barrel is unloaded, slide the rod down the barrel and make a witness mark on the ramrod. Note the position of the mark when the barrel is empty and when the barrel is charged with powder and bullet. If your mark falls anywhere between those two points, it means that you've forgotten powder or the bullet in the loading process.

Prior to loading, fire one cap to make sure the nipple orifice is open and your firing pin will fully strike the cap. Drop a pre-measured charge down the barrel. A suggested load would be two 50-grain pellets of Pyrodex or Triple Seven. With the palm of your hand, rap the breech of the gun to settle the powder. Then start your bullet by mounting it in the barrel crown, using the pressure of your thumb to get it started. Use a bullet starter to push the bullet down the barrel a few

inches. Use the ramrod to seat the bullet against the powder charge. Note the position of your Witness Mark.

Set the rifle safety to the "safe" position, open the bolt and push the cap into the nipple. The gun is ready to fire.

## Sighting In with a Clean Barrel

Many muzzleloaders are capable of putting three shots within a 1-inch (2.5 cm) group at 100 yards (91 m). When sighting-in, you must wipe your barrel between each shot. I keep an extra rod beside me on the shooting bench. After each shot, I wipe the barrel with a clean, damp patch.

After sighting-in at 25 yards (22.75 m), place a target at 100 yards. Consider zeroing your rifle to strike 3 inches (7.6 cm) high at 100 yards. With my pet load combination—100 grains of Triple Seven and a 260-grain saboted bullet—my bullets strike 3 inches high at 100, 3 inches low at 150 (136.5 m), 6 inches (15 cm) low at 175 (159 m), and 12 inches (30 cm) low at 200 yards (182 m). I tape my ballistics chart to the stock for quick reference.

At the range, after firing twenty to thirty shots, remove the breech plug and give the rifle a thorough cleaning. Put a small amount of anti-seize grease on the threads of your breech plug to make the next removal an easy one.

## Get Fouled

Because the gun is sighted-in with a fouled barrel, it should be hunted with a fouled barrel. A shot from a cleaned barrel impacts in a slightly different place than a shot fired from a fouled barrel. Shoot a fouling shot prior to target practice or the hunt. Simply fire a half load and a bullet into a safe backstop such as a dirt bank.

There is no need to clean the rifle after the fouling shot. When using Triple Seven, you may leave the barrel fouled for the duration of the hunt. When using blackpowder, you need to clean the barrel every evening. Your fouled barrel gives the consistent velocity needed for on-target performance, when the shot counts.

## 45 VS. 50 VS. 54

All states and provinces that have seasons for black bear have mandated minimum requirements for caliber of the rifle and the bullet. Contact local state or provincial game departments for information on muzzleloader seasons.

The state of Alaska requires a minimum of a 50-caliber rifle for hunting bear, for good reason. The heavier bullet is more likely to break bone and do the kind of tissue damage that puts the bear down fast. In some states, 40-caliber is the minimum allowable size for hunting all big game, including bears. At best, this is a compromise.

When in pursuit of black bear, I want at least a 50-caliber bullet with enough weight to finish the job at the first shot. A heavier bullet is more likely to retain enough energy to carry through the animal, leave a bigger wound channel and a better blood trail.

— Gary Lewis

## Sights

A scope extends the long-range reach of most shooters and is the best way to realize the rifle's potential. Depending on the load combination, a shooter should be able to make shots at 150 yards (137 m) and beyond with complete confidence.

Most rifles are drilled and tapped for scope mounts. Installing an optics system is simple. Mounts are available from Warne, Weaver, and other manufacturers to allow quick installation of your scope.

Because most game taken with a muzzleloader is encountered at ranges between 10 yards (9.1 m) and 100 yards (91 m), the overwhelming choice of most muzzleloaders is a low-range variable scope, adjustable from 1x to 6x. For game, big or small, you simply don't need more magnification on a muzzleloading rifle.

In practice, take shots at ranges of 100 yards, 125 yards (113.75 m) and so on, out to 200 yards (182 m). Record the bullet drop and make notes on ballistics performance. This type of homework pays dividends on the hunt.

## The Follow-Up Shot

With a muzzleloader, most game is taken on the first shot. A second shot is rarely required. There are times, however, when a follow-up shot is necessary to dispatch a wounded animal. If you carry a pre-loaded speedloader, you can be ready to shoot again in 15 seconds or less. Carry between two and five speedloaders, charged and ready to go. And practice using them—loading and firing with speed and accuracy.

Gary Lewis with a recurve bow at the summit of one of his favorite ridges. When hunting with traditional gear, shots must be taken at close range or not at all.

## BOWHUNTING

Taking a bear with bent stick and string is one of archery's greatest accomplishments. A lot of bow hunters take to the woods in pursuit of bear over bait or to spot-and-stalk Mr. Big. For most, the bow used for whitetail back east or elk out west will be the tool of choice. At close range, with a sharp broadhead and a heavy arrow, a 50-pound (22 kg) or heavier bow is a deadly weapon. One well-placed arrow is all it takes to put a bear down.

Getting to that moment when the arrow is released is what the bear hunt is all about. A tree stand is the overwhelming choice that most hunters opt for when hunting over bait. The height of the stand puts the archer at an advantage, but bears do climb trees and more than one hunter has been stalked in his tree by a curious, hungry or enraged bruin. One thing to consider is the fact that, from a distance of 20 feet (6 m) in the air, the animal's heart/lung area is partially hidden by its spine and rib cage. For this reason,

some hunters opt to hunt from a ground blind. Arrows shot from the ground are more apt to penetrate deeper for quicker kills.

A rifle hunter can pick up his rifle a week before the season starts, take a few shots, confirm that he can still hit point of aim and be ready for opening day. An archer, on the other hand, should start shooting his or her bow at least five months before the season opener.

Archery tackle is highly personal equipment. What works well for one hunter may not work at all for another. Differences in stature, strength and preferences make each bow setup unique to the individual who put it together. For this reason, the hunter new to archery should listen to the advice of veteran archers but make decisions based on their own personal preferences.

"Bear Man" Bateman used a bow to take this bear. Many archers, when hunting bear for the first time, opt to hunt from a tree stand over bait.

To take a bear cleanly with a bow, arrow placement must be precise. Only practice will prepare the hunter to make the shot when it is presented.

## Compound or Traditional?

Most archers use compound bows. The advantage is the draw weight let-off used to hold the bow at full draw. A longbow or a recurve takes 60 pounds (27 kg) to hold at draw length, but a compound bow set at the same weight may only require 21 pounds (9.45 kg) to keep it at full draw. Another advantage of the compound is the ease with which it can be accessorized. With bolt-on components, the compound bow is easily fitted with sights, a quiver, a rest, a string peep sight, a stabilizer and recoil reducers. Today, most compound shooters prefer to use a trigger-actuated release for consistency. The technology has allowed archers to shoot faster with better accuracy than ever before.

Some compound shooters have switched back to traditional equipment to experience what they call a purer form of archery. Longbows are the most difficult to shoot well. Recurves, with their double-flexed limbs, deliver more energy to the arrow and less shock to the shooter's forearm.

Space-age or traditional, the best place to start is at an archery store. The dealer will let you try a bow to determine draw length and then assess your physical strength to decide how heavy a bow you can pull.

## The Arrow and Broadhead

The arrow is the most important piece of the archer's tackle. It must deliver the energy of the bow in a consistent manner, shot after shot, with the broadhead flying straight and true. To accomplish this, the arrow is spined for flex and is matched to the archer's draw length. Fletching may be either feather or plastic. Most compound shooters prefer plastic vanes, but feathered fletching shoots better through some rests. Many traditional shooters prefer the more forgiving feather fletches.

For a substantial quarry like a bear, a heavier arrow is preferred to carry the energy and the broadhead through the animal. With an arrow, the bear is killed not by shock as with a bullet, but by hemorrhage. That leads us to the broadhead. It should be the same weight as the practice field tip and it should be constructed to break bone with the tip and slice through hair, skin and organs with its razor sharp blades.

Preparing for his bear hunt, Darrin Isaak shot his target at a variety of distances and from many different angles. When bowhunting, distance judging and precise arrow placement is critical.

For an archer, there is only one good target on a bear. The animal should be standing broadside or slightly quartering away and the arrow should be directed right behind the shoulder into the vital heart/lung area. With a good hit, the bear leaves a wide blood trail, bleeding out of both sides of the body.

Once you purchase your new bow then it is time to start shooting. Take a few lessons first to ensure that muscles are properly trained for draw, hold and release. Consistency is the most important part of the practice routine. Your archery store may have a shooting range or, better yet, you can set one up in your own backyard. Shooting every day at known distances will help you to understand your limitations and enable you to judge distances accurately.

Take shots from a kneeling position as well as standing. Shoot uphill and downhill to learn how you and your equipment perform under a variety of conditions. Practice while wearing the same clothes that you will be hunting in. Will you wear gloves or a head net while hunting? Your shot will change if you put these on for the first time on opening day instead of practicing with them on in the preseason.

When hunting from a tree stand, the higher above the ground the stand is positioned, the steeper the angle of the shot. The steeper the angle, the trickier the shot for the archer, because the bear's spine protects the vitals. A better shot is made from the ground or just off the ground to allow the arrow to penetrate both lungs.

Informal "stump shoots" and organized events, like the popular 3-D courses, will polish your shooting skills and help you make those little adjustments in equipment and technique that can mean the difference between putting bear meat in the stew pot or buying the neat little shrink-wrapped packages at the butcher store.

## PLANNING CHECKLIST

Directional wind indicator
Cover scent
Binoculars
Spotting scope
Laser range finder
Knife
Back-up knife
Whetstone
Rifle
20-rounds ammunition
Calls
Survival gear
Unit or county maps
Topographic maps
Compass
Global Positioning System (GPS) unit
Rope
Come-along or winch
T-Hanger and tackle for skinning
Game bags
Camera
Surveyor's tape
Canteen
Extra batteries for all electronics

Wayne Endicott (top) arrowed this black bear on a spring hunt. This archer's favorite tactic is to spot the bears first, close the distance then use a call to bring the bear into bow range.

A bow is a highly personal piece of equipment and, often, must be tuned to the individual who will use it (bottom). It's important to handle a number of bows before making a final decision to purchase.

# CHAPTER FIVE

# After the Shot

If the bullet or the arrow went true to its mark, chances are good that the bear will be piled up within 50 yards (45.5 m). But if the shot hit the bear in the liver or broke its leg, it may take longer to locate the dead bear. Watch the bear's reaction to the strike for clues to the hit and the trail. Waiting 20 minutes before beginning to track is a good ballpark timeframe.

## TRACKING

If the animal jumped at the shot, the bullet probably went too low. There may be a few hairs if the bullet creased its belly. Hit in the paunch, a bear hunches up and heads for cover. If there is blood, digested food and quite a bit of hair, you have hit the animal low in the belly. Give the animal time to lie down and stiffen up. It won't run far if it isn't chased. You may just find it in the thickest cover in the area.

If the animal dropped, you may have made a perfect shot, but don't go looking for it until you have chambered another round. If the skull was creased or a vertebra was nicked, the bear might just be unconscious. Be ready, because your trophy may go bounding away while your partner slaps you on the back.

If there is no indication of a hit, investigate anyway. You owe it to the bear and to yourself. You may find hair at the site. Follow the tracks. More than once, I have followed up animals that I thought had escaped just to find them piled up 100 yards (91 m) away.

Likely, there's a trophy at the end of this trail, but it could also be a wounded bear that has hooked around and is waiting to ambush the hunter.

Bear hit in the liver leave dark blood on the trail. Do your best to find it. The animal will die in less than an hour. Bear can be hit in the brisket, or the fleshy parts of the legs and still survive. But every effort should be made to recover the animal. Sometimes there is enough blood from such hits to allow the hunter to follow and get in position for another shot.

I always tie orange flagging to the spot I am standing after I shoot. Next, I tie a ribbon to the spot where the animal stood at the shot. Then I work out the trail. At first blood and every patch or turn in the spoor, I leave another ribbon. This helps me work out the general line of travel. I track faster this way and am able to return to the trail if I lose the sign.

A word of caution: A wounded bear may double back on its own tracks. On a hunt in Prince William Sound, I found the tracks of a bear that had been shot through the body. It had been bleeding out of both sides and its tracks led up through a muskeg then hooked right into the willows and devil's club. The bear had climbed the hill, turned in a couple of circles, then followed a high trail back toward the beach. We lost the bear's trail in the devil's club where he'd lain in ambush for his tormentors. Along the whole trail, we never found a boot track. Whoever had shot him hadn't followed his trail.

## How Big Is That Bear?

A lot of first time bear hunters are looking for a big one. They hear about 5-footers (1.5 m), 6-footers (1.8 m), and 7-footers (2 m). They hear about 300-pound (135 kg) bears, 400-pound (180 kg) bears, 500-pound (225 kg) bears and bigger. They hear about skulls that are 18-inchers (46 cm), 19-inchers (48 cm), and 20-inchers (51 cm). And if they go somewhere beyond their home state to hunt, someplace legendary for big bears like Maine or Minnesota or Alaska, they expect to see big bears, but they don't know what a big bear looks like.

For someone who has never hunted bear, it is hard to understand what a big bear looks like in the field. We measure a bear's size in four different ways. The first one is by weight. This is difficult, because the same bear's weight may vary by as much as 30 percent from spring to fall. And most people who kill a bear never weigh it, but they are still quick to say that the bear was a 400- or 500-pounder (180 or 225 kg).

A better way is to measure the animal from the tip of its nose to the tip of its tail before it is skinned. The biggest sows generally do not exceed a measurement of 5 feet, 6 inches (1.7 m). A good bear will fall between 5 feet (1.5 m) and 6 feet (1.8 m) long. The bigger boars measure from 6 feet (1.8 m) to 7 feet, 6 inches (2.3 m), or more.

A third way is to square the bear. Take a measurement from the tip of the nose to the end of the tail then measure from the tips of the outstretched front legs from claw to claw. Add the total and divide by two. A good bear will square around 5 feet, 8 inches (1.8 m). The biggest bears could square anywhere from 6 feet, 6 inches (2 m) to close to 8 feet (2.4 m).

The fourth way is by measuring the skull. With a caliper, the cleaned skull is measured from front to back and from side to side for a total score measured in inches. Skull sizes vary, but in general, an average bear's skull will run between 17 and 18 inches (43 and 46 cm), while a very big bear's skull may stretch the calipers to 20 inches (51 cm).

## FIELD CARE

You've shot and tracked your bear. Now the hard work begins. This is the point when you need the answer to the question, "What am I going to do with my bear?" You might go for a standing life-size mount, or maybe you want the bear on all

fours. Then again, a wall-mount half life-size might be a better choice. Perhaps a shoulder mount would do.

The hide can be made into a rug, with or without the head. For some people, a tanned hide is enough. Others want a felt or blanket backing with rings sewn in for hanging on the wall. A hide may also be turned into a vest, or made into a coat or a quiver. The bleached skull with teeth bared makes for great shock value back home or at the office.

The time to decide is now, with the bear on the ground. Sometimes the animal's condition makes the difference. Some hides are rubbed and don't make the best rugs. Whatever you decide to do with the bear, you'll want to keep some records. They may come in handy later. Start with the camera. You may want pictures of the paws and of the head from different angles.

Doug Evans used an Austin & Halleck muzzleloader on this hunt over bait in Minnesota.

With a bear down in the last minutes of the day, flashlights and headlamps make the work easier and can mean the difference between spending the night with the bear in the woods and finding the way out to the truck and a hot meal at camp.

## Measuring

Take pictures first then go to work with a tape measure for five basic measurements. Start with the distance from the inside corner of the eye to the tip of the nose. Second, measure from the tip of the nose to the back of the skull. Third, measure the circumference of the neck behind the ears. Fourth, measure the length of the body from the tip of the nose to the base of the tail. Last, measure the body around the middle.

## Dressing

The next step is to field dress the animal. You'll find out soon enough why most experts recommend you bring two knives. You may wish you had three before it's finished. Save the smallest blade for the detail work.

Shoulder-length rubber gloves are a big help at this stage. Tie off the penis (if the bear is a male) to keep urine from fouling the meat. Start at the genitals or between the legs and cut away the skin and muscle tissue to open the body cavity all the way to the sternum. Tip the entrails out and reach up as far inside the rib cage as you can go and cut away the windpipe and tissue. Beneath the tail, cut out the anus and pull it back into the body and let it slide out onto the gut pile. Now the meat will cool from the inside while you skin the animal.

## Skinning

For a shoulder mount, skin the bear in the way you'd prepare a deer head. Cut in a circle around the body, starting at the sternum then split along the spine and run the blade up between the ears. Cape to the ears and skin out the face, or stop and leave the detail work for the taxidermist.

For a rug or a full mount, the primary work is the same. With the animal on its back, finish the belly cut by opening the skin from the sternum to within 2 inches (5 cm) of the chin. On the other end, cut from between the legs out to the base of the tail.

Skinning out the legs is the tricky part. Make the cuts at the line where hairlines grow in opposite directions. Mess this up a little bit and the taxidermist can fix it. Botch the job and you might as well make a vest out of the hide.

Along the back of the rear legs, follow the line where the short hair meets the longer hair all the way to the anus. Mirror that cut on the other rear leg. Whatever you do, you probably won't need the foot pads from the rear feet. You can cut down the center of the pad and discard it later.

Now move to the front legs. Turn the front leg so that the pad is pointed at the sky. Begin your cut just above the pad and work the blade straight to the point opposite the elbow. Here's where it gets a little dicey. Don't continue in a straight line. Instead, turn the blade toward the middle of the armpit to intersect the center cut at a right angle.

All your cuts on one side of the animal must be mirrored on the other side or the taxidermist is going to get grumpy. Grumpy taxidermists tend to charge more to balance unbalanced bear skins.

Skin out from your cuts, taking care to remove excess fat and to not cut the hide. For a full-size or half life-size mount, you'll want to keep the front pads. For a rug you don't need them. In any case, you can leave them on and let the taxidermist do the tricky work. Break the leg at the joint and cut it away, leaving the paws attached to the hide. Do the same thing with the back feet.

This representative of the Alaska Fish and Wildlife Department is checking a fresh hide for the tattoos the agency uses to mark problem bears. This bear has no more problems.

Skinning over the head, stop when you get to the lumps, which are the insides of the ears. Here, you decide whether to cape out the face or leave the head on and let the taxidermist do it. This could depend on how far you are from the taxidermist and your skill with the caping knife.

Separate the ear lumps from the skull by running the blade as close as possible to the bone. Go careful to the bear's eyes and cheeks. From the fur side stick your finger into the eye socket as a guide. Ease through the membrane around the eye as close to the skull as possible and then slice through the cheek muscle to reveal the teeth.

Continue toward the nose. Leave the lips on the hide rather than on the skull. At the nose, you'll find a section of cartilage. Cut through this and the hide is off the bear.

Freeze the hide now or salt it in preparation for the taxidermist. You'll want the hide in the freezer or in the taxidermist's care within two days to prevent hair slippage. If this is impossible, skin out the lips with a small pocketknife and turn out the ears and nose. Then turn out the paws. Next, remove as much of the flesh from the hide as possible and thoroughly coat all the inner surfaces with salt. It may take 10 to 25 pounds (4.5 to 11 kg) of salt to put away a black bear hide. Use un-iodized salt. Rub it in then roll or fold it, flesh to flesh. After a day or two, hang it in the shade to drain. Then resalt and refold.

If you want to do it right the first time, spend a half-hour with your taxidermist prior to the hunt. And take these instructions with you in the field.

Proper care of the hide prevents hair slippage. The hide should be frozen or taken to the taxidermist within 48 hours.

# A FEW RECIPES

Some people prefer the meat of a spring bear to a fall bear. While others prefer the fall bear to the spring. In truth, flavor and quality depends a great deal on what the bear has been eating in the last few weeks. Coastal bears may retain the flavors of fall salmon runs even into the early spring.

Grasses, grubs, berries, and fruit tend to sweeten the meat, while a diet of carrion and salmon tends to make the meat greasier. Bear meat is leaner than most meats with a texture that has been compared to pork. In the frying pan, it tends to be darker than beef or venison.

## Bear Stew

1¹/₂ to 2 pounds (0.7 to 0.9 kg) bear
   stew meat
¹/₄ cup (62 ml) all-purpose flour
1 teaspoon (5 ml) dried marjoram leaves
1 teaspoon (5 ml) salt
¹/₈ teaspoon (0.6 ml) pepper
2 tablespoons (30 ml) vegetable oil
1 can (16 ounce/475 ml) whole tomatoes, undrained
1 cup (250 ml) water
¹/₄ cup (62 ml) white wine or water
1 tablespoon (15 ml) vinegar
1 medium onion, cut in half lengthwise
   and thinly sliced
¹/₂ cup (125 ml) chopped celery
2 cloves garlic, minced
1 bay leaf
2 medium baking potatoes

4 to 6 servings

Remove all fat and silverskin from meat. Cut into 1-inch (2.5 cm) pieces. In large plastic food-storage bag, combine flour, marjoram, salt, and pepper; shake to mix. Add meat; shake to coat. In heavy medium saucepan, heat oil over medium-high heat until hot. Add meat and flour mixture. Brown, stirring occasionally. Add remaining ingredients except potatoes; mix well. Heat to boiling. Reduce heat; cover. Simmer 1 hour, stirring occasionally.

Cut potatoes into 1-inch (2.5 cm) chunks. Add to saucepan. Heat to boiling. Reduce heat; cover. Simmer until meat and potatoes are tender, about 1 hour, stirring occasionally. Discard bay leaf before serving.

## Big-Game Pie

Double Pie Crust Pastry:
2 cups (500 ml) all-purpose flour
1 teaspoon (5 ml) salt
2/3 cup (160 ml) shortening
3 tablespoons (50 ml) butter or margarine,
    room temperature
5 to 7 tablespoons (75 to 100 ml) cold water

Filling:
2 cups (455 g) cut-up cooked big game
1 1/2 cups (375 ml) thinly sliced potato
1/2 cup (125 ml) thinly sliced carrot
1/2 cup (125 ml) cubed rutabaga, 1/2-inch
    (2.5 cm) cubes
1 small onion, thinly sliced and
    separated into rings
1 package (0.75 ounce/21 ml) herb-flavored
    brown gravy mix, or 1 cup (250 ml) leftover
    game gravy
1/4 teaspoon (1.25 ml) salt
1/8 teaspoon (0.6 ml) pepper
1 tablespoon (15 ml) butter or margarine,
    cut up

Glaze (optional):
1 egg
1 tablespoon (15 ml) water

4 to 6 servings

Heat oven to 375°F (190°C). Combine flour and salt in medium mixing bowl. Cut shortening and 3 tablespoons (50 ml) butter into flour until particles resemble coarse crumbs. Sprinkle flour mixture with cold water while tossing with fork, until particles just cling together. Divide into two balls. Roll one ball on lightly floured board into thin circle at least 2 inches (5 cm) larger than inverted 9-inch (23 cm) pie plate. Fit pastry into pie plate. Trim overhang. Set other ball aside.

Layer meat, potato, carrot, rutabaga, and onion in pastry shell. Prepare gravy mix according to package directions, adding 1/4 teaspoon (1.25 ml) salt and the pepper. Pour into pie. Dot pie filling with butter.

Roll out remaining pastry. Place on filling. Seal and flute edges. If desired, roll out pastry scraps; cut into decorations and place on pastry top. Cut several slits in pastry top. In small bowl, blend glaze ingredients. Brush over pastry top. Bake until crust is golden brown, about 1 hour. Let stand 10 minutes before serving.

## Brad's Swiss Steak

1½ pounds (0.7 kg) boneless bear round steak,
½ to 1 inch (1.25 to 2.5 cm) thick
⅓ cup (83 ml) all-purpose flour
1 teaspoon (5 ml) salt
¼ teaspoon (1.25 ml) pepper
3 to 4 tablespoons (50 to 60 ml) bacon fat
1 can (16 ounce/475 ml) stewed tomatoes
¾ cup (185 ml) water
1 teaspoon (5 ml) instant beef bouillon granules
½ teaspoon (2.5 ml) dried basil leaves
½ teaspoon (2.5 ml) dried marjoram leaves
1 medium onion, thinly sliced

4 to 6 servings

Trim meat; cut into serving-sized pieces. Pound to
¼- to ½-inch (0.6 to 1.25 cm) thickness with meat
mallet. On a sheet of waxed paper, mix flour, salt,
and pepper. Dip steaks in flour mixture, turning to
coat. In large skillet, heat bacon fat over medium
heat. Add coated steaks; brown lightly on both
sides. Fry in two batches if necessary. In small
mixing bowl, mix stewed tomatoes, water, bouillon granules, basil, and marjoram; pour over
steaks. Top meat and tomatoes with sliced onion.
Heat to boiling. Reduce heat; cover. Simmer over
very low heat until meat is tender, 1½ to 2 hours.
Skim fat if desired.

## Lum's Sweet Bear Manapua
*Courtesy Tod Lum, Oregon*

2 pounds (0.9 kg) shredded bear meat
sweet Chinese BBQ marinade
6 homemade rolls

Marinate shredded bear meat in sweet Chinese
BBQ sauce overnight. Make homemade rolls and
stuff with the marinated bear meat. Steam for 30
minutes and serve.

6 servings

## Crock Pot Goodness— Braun's Game Burger Chili
*Courtesy Sheila Braun, Oregon*

1 can (16-ounce/475 ml) drained black beans
1 can (16-ounce/475 ml) drained kidney beans
2 cans (14.5 ounce/864 ml) stewed tomatoes
½ pound (0.2 kg) browned bear burger
½ cup (125 ml) chopped onion
1 clove garlic
2 teaspoons (10 ml) chili powder
1 teaspoon (5 ml) pepper
1 teaspoon (5 ml) cumin
salt to taste

4 servings

Put all ingredients in a slow cooker in order of the
ingredient list. Stir occasionally.

Cover and cook on Low, 10 to 12 hours.

## Cabbage Patch Steamer Bear
*Courtesy Tod Lum, Oregon*

2-pound (0.9 kg) bear roast
4 ti leaves from Kauai
Hawaiian salt
½ pound (225 g) cabbage
¼ pound (15 g) sweet onions

4 servings

Sprinkle bear roast with a generous helping
of Hawaiian salt and wrap it in leaves. Cover
completely in foil. Cook in a steamer for 8
hours. Stir fry with cabbage and sweet onions.

"When removed from foil, the meat falls
off the bones and shreds easily. It is moist
and flavorful like a Hawaiian roast pig."
–Tod Lum

## Bear Steak Flamade

$^{1}$/3 cup (83 ml) all-purpose flour
1 teaspoon (5 ml) salt
$^{1}$/4 teaspoon (1.25 ml)pepper
2 pounds (0.9 kg) bear round steak,
    1 inch (2.5 cm) thick
$^{1}$/2 cup (125 ml) butter or margarine, divided
2 tablespoons (30 ml) olive oil or
    vegetable oil
4 medium onions, thinly sliced
1$^{1}$/2 cups (375 ml) beer
$^{1}$/4 teaspoon (1.25 ml) dried
    marjoram leaves
$^{1}$/4 teaspoon (1.25 ml) dried
    thyme leaves
1 bay leaf

6 to 8 servings

Heat oven to 325°F (165°C). On a sheet of waxed paper, mix flour, salt, and pepper. Dip steak in flour mixture, turning to coat. In large skillet, melt $^{1}$/4 cup (62 ml) butter in oil over medium-low heat. Add steak; brown on both sides over medium-high heat. Transfer meat and drippings to 3-quart (3 liter) casserole; set aside.

In large skillet, melt remaining $^{1}$/4 cup (62 ml) butter over medium-low heat. Add onions, stirring to coat with butter. Cover. Cook until tender but not brown, about 10 minutes. Pour onions over steak in casserole. Add remaining ingredients. Cover. Bake until meat is tender, 2 to 2$^{1}$/2 hours. Discard bay leaf before serving.

## Big-Game Pot Roast

1/3 cup (83 ml) all-purpose flour
1 teaspoon (5 ml) dried basil leaves
1/2 teaspoon (2.5 ml) dried marjoram leaves
1/2 teaspoon (2.5 ml) dried thyme leaves
1/2 teaspoon (2.5 ml) salt
1/4 teaspoon (1.25 ml) pepper
2 1/2- to 3-pound (1 to 1.3 kg) bear roast
3 tablespoons (15 ml) vegetable oil
1 can (10 1/2 ounce/300 ml) condensed
   French onion soup
1/2 cup (125 ml) water, broth, or wine
1 bay leaf
1 rutabaga, peeled and cut into 1-inch
   (2.5 cm) cubes
4 to 6 medium carrots, cut into 2-inch
   (5 cm) pieces
3 stalks celery, cut into 2-inch (5 cm) pieces

4 to 6 servings

Heat oven to 350°F (180°C).

In large plastic food-storage bag, combine flour, basil, marjoram, thyme, salt, and pepper; shake to mix. Add meat; shake to coat. In Dutch oven, brown meat on both sides in oil. Add remaining flour mixture, soup, water, and bay leaf.

Heat to boiling. Remove from heat; cover. Bake for 1 1/2 hours. Add rutabaga, carrots, and celery. Recover. Bake until meat and vegetables are tender, 1 to 1 1/2 hours longer.

Discard bay leaf before serving.

# The Future of Bear Hunting

By Gary Lewis

I needed a few last minute items before I left for Montana: game bags, MREs, and film for the camera. I like to frequent stores that carry one or more of my books, so I stopped in at a local department store and headed back for the sporting goods section.

While I was standing at the gun counter, a little boy walked up. He was about five years old and was wearing a puffy coat because it was cold outside. His mother pushed a shopping cart with his little sister riding in the seat. Mother looked bored, but she wanted some help in the automotive department and so she was looking for someone in sporting goods.

The little boy in the puffy coat was looking at the guns and the taxidermy. He extended his arm and pointed at the bearskin rug. "Someday," he said, "I'm going to buy a gun and shoot a bear. Then I'm going to put it on the wall."

I smiled. I remembered thinking the same thing when I was about his age. But mother did not look impressed. "You are not," she said.

"Yes, I'm going to buy a gun and shoot a bear. Then I'm going to put it on the wall."

The boy looked around to see who might have heard him. When our eyes met, I gave him a "thumbs up" and smiled. He turned back around and looked at his mom.

Mother gave me a withering look. "He's not going to be a hunter."

I laughed. Probably louder and longer than I should have.

She was exasperated. "I'm not a hunter, his dad's not a hunter, he's not going to be a hunter."

Then I told her. "That's funny, that's what my mom said, a long time ago." My dad quit hunting when I was nine and my mom never encouraged it. She wanted me to be a fisherman, not a hunter. But hunting was something I had to do.

The boy's mother was standing right in front of the rack that held my first book, *Hunting Oregon*. I walked over and pulled it out. "And now," I said, "I write books about it." I let her take a long look at the cover, so she would know what to buy the little boy for Christmas.

As I left the store, I wondered how we, as hunters, can reach that little boy. Then I realized he has already been reached. Whoever decided that department store should have a gun counter. Whoever decided that a bearskin rug and deer heads should be part of the decoration. Whoever decided that they would sell hunting and fishing items in that store. They were the ones that reached that little boy in the puffy coat. They had planted the seed of outdoor adventure in his young heart. It's up to us to nourish it.

Twelve-year-old Jennifer Lewis with the bear she took on the second day of her first big game hunt.

On a spring bear hunt, there are many opportunities to instruct a young hunter in all aspects of the chase.

Nathan Endicott with his first black bear. Where bears are numerous, a young bowhunter can get a lot of chances by playing the wind, stalking close and using a predator call.

# Resources

**Bear Hunting magazine**

Jeffrey Folsom, Publisher
www.bear-hunting.com
subscriptions@bear-hunting.com
(320) 743-6600

**North American Bear Foundation**

Brian Bachman
www.nabf.org
nabf@nabf.org
(218) 828-7739

**National Rifle Association of America**

www.NRA.org
(877) 672-2000

**U.S. Sportsmen's Alliance**

www.ussportsmen.org

**Safari Club International**

www.SafariClub.org
(520) 620-1220

**Rocky Mountain Elk Foundation**

www.elkfoundation.org
(800) CALL-ELK

# Contributing Manufacturers

Warne Scope Mounts
800.683.5590
www.warnescopemounts.com

Gerber Legendary Blades
800.950.6161
www.gerberblades.com

Nosler, Inc.
541.382.3921
www.nosler.com

Power Belt Bullets
www.powerbeltbullets.com

CVA
770.449.4687
www.cva.com

Alpen
909.987.8370
www.alpenoutdoor.com

Bushnell
www.bushnell.com

Hodgdon
913.362.9455
www.hodgdon.com

Ruger
www.ruger.com

Blackhawk
www.blackhawk.com

Fox Pro
www.gofoxpro.com

Buck Bomb
866.850.6653
www.buckbomb.com

New Line Products
800.542.4645
www.newlineproducts.com

Federal Ammunition
www.atk.com

Bear Near
www.rockcove.com

Quake Industries
www.quakeinc.com

Security Equipment Corporation
800.325.9568

Bear Scents, LLC
www.bearscents.com

Little Smokey
www.rockcove.com

# Index

# Photo Credits

# Creative Publishing international
## Your Complete Source of How-to Information for the Outdoors

### Hunting Books
- Advanced Turkey Hunting
- Advanced Whitetail Hunting
- Bowhunting Equipment & Skills
- Bowhunter's Guide to Accurate Shooting
- The Complete Guide to Hunting
- Dog Training
- Elk Hunting
- How to Think Like a Survivor
- Hunting Record-Book Bucks
- Mule Deer Hunting
- Muzzleloading
- Outdoor Guide to Using Your GPS
- Pronghorn Hunting
- Waterfowl Hunting
- Whitetail Hunting
- Whitetail Techniques & Tactics
- Wild Turkey

### Fishing Books
- Advanced Bass Fishing
- The Art of Freshwater Fishing
- The Complete Guide to Freshwater Fishing
- Fishing for Catfish

- Fishing Rivers & Streams
- Fishing Tips & Tricks
- Fishing with Artificial Lures
- Inshore Salt Water Fishing
- Kids Gone Campin'
- Kids Gone Fishin'
- Largemouth Bass
- Live Bait Fishing
- Modern Methods of Ice Fishing
- Northern Pike & Muskie
- Offshore Salt Water Fishing
- Panfish
- Salt Water Fishing Tactics
- Smallmouth Bass
- Striped Bass Fishing: Salt Water Strategies
- Successful Walleye Fishing
- Trout
- Ultralight Fishing

### Fly Fishing Books
- The Art of Fly Tying
- The Art of Fly Tying – CD ROM
- Complete Photo Guide to Fly Fishing
- Complete Photo Guide to Fly Tying

- Fishing Dry Flies
- Fishing Nymphs, Wet Flies & Streamers
- Fly-Fishing Equipment & Skills
- Fly Fishing for Beginners
- Fly Fishing for Trout in Streams
- Fly-Tying Techniques & Patterns

### Cookbooks
- All-Time Favorite Game Bird Recipes
- America's Favorite Fish Recipes
- America's Favorite Wild Game Recipes
- Backyard Grilling
- Cooking Wild in Kate's Camp
- Cooking Wild in Kate's Kitchen
- Dressing & Cooking Wild Game
- The New Cleaning & Cooking Fish
- Preparing Fish & Wild Game
- The Saltwater Cookbook
- Venison Cookery
- The Wild Butcher

To purchase these or other Creative Publishing international titles,
contact your local bookseller, or visit our website at
**www.creativepub.com**

*The Complete* FLY FISHERMAN™